America, where the magic of diversity intertwines like the colors of a rainbow, and every child is a bright spark in the grand adventure of our shared dreams!

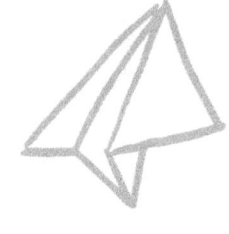
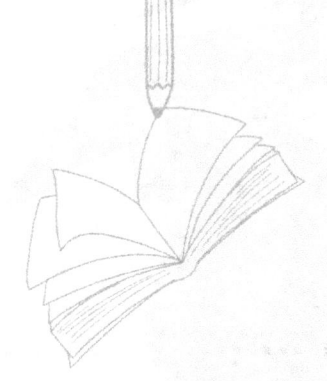
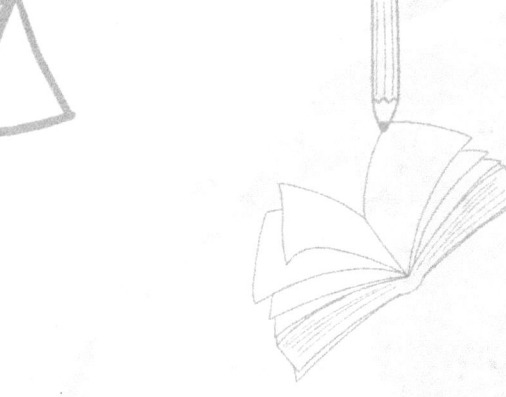
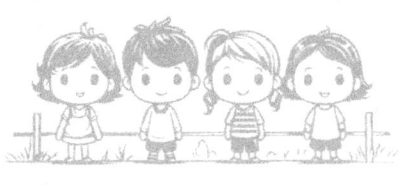
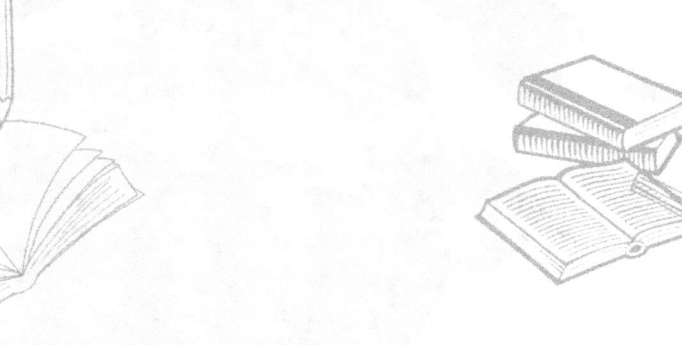
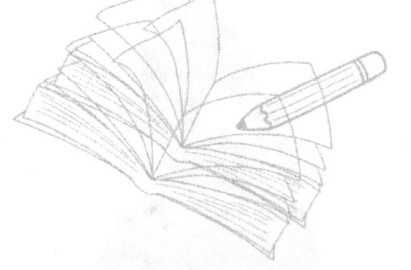
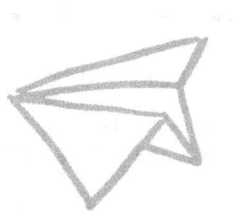
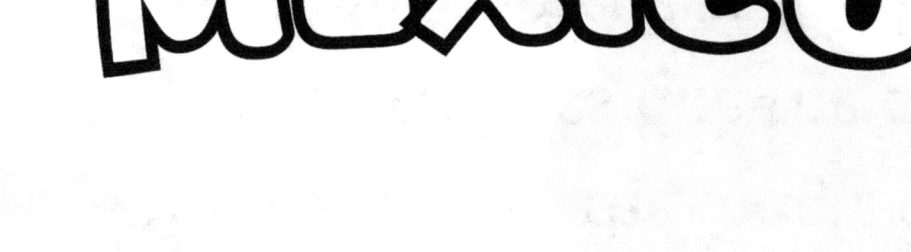
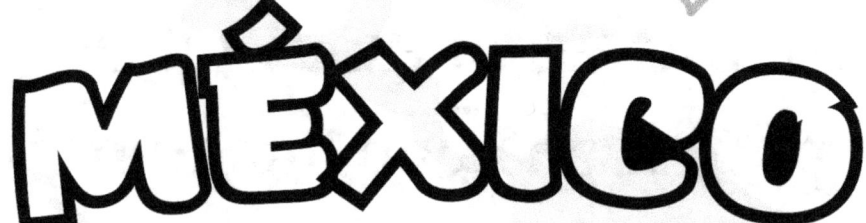

MÉXICO

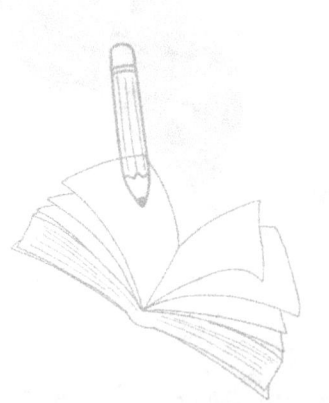
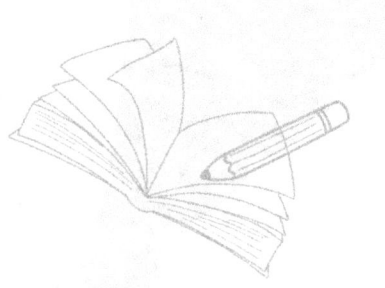
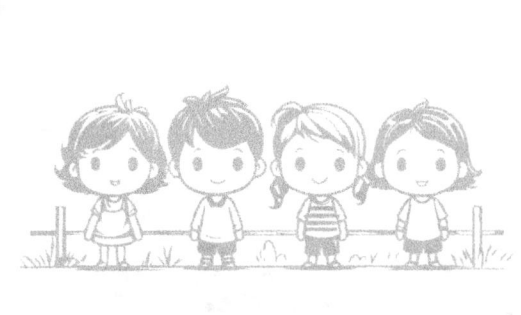

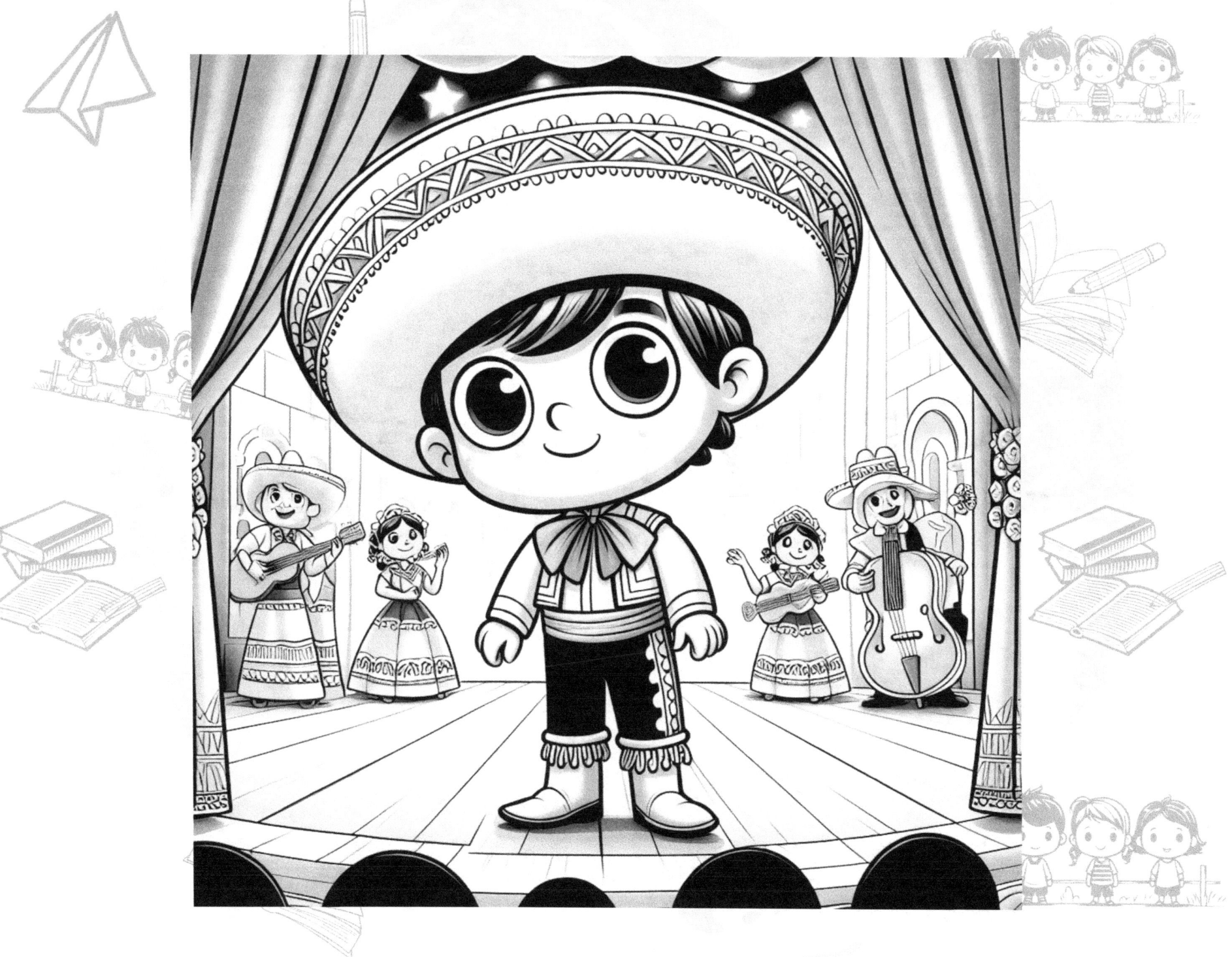

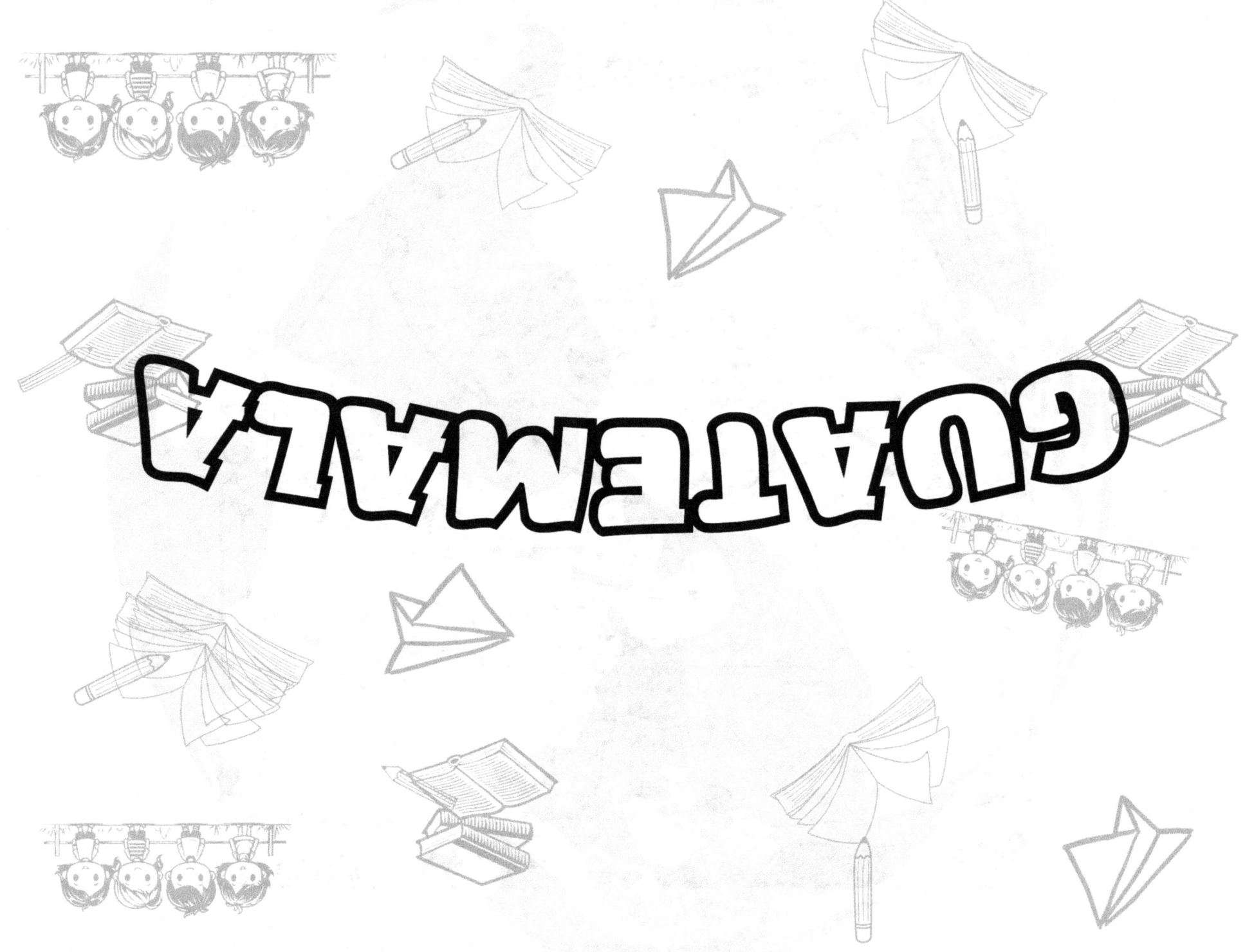

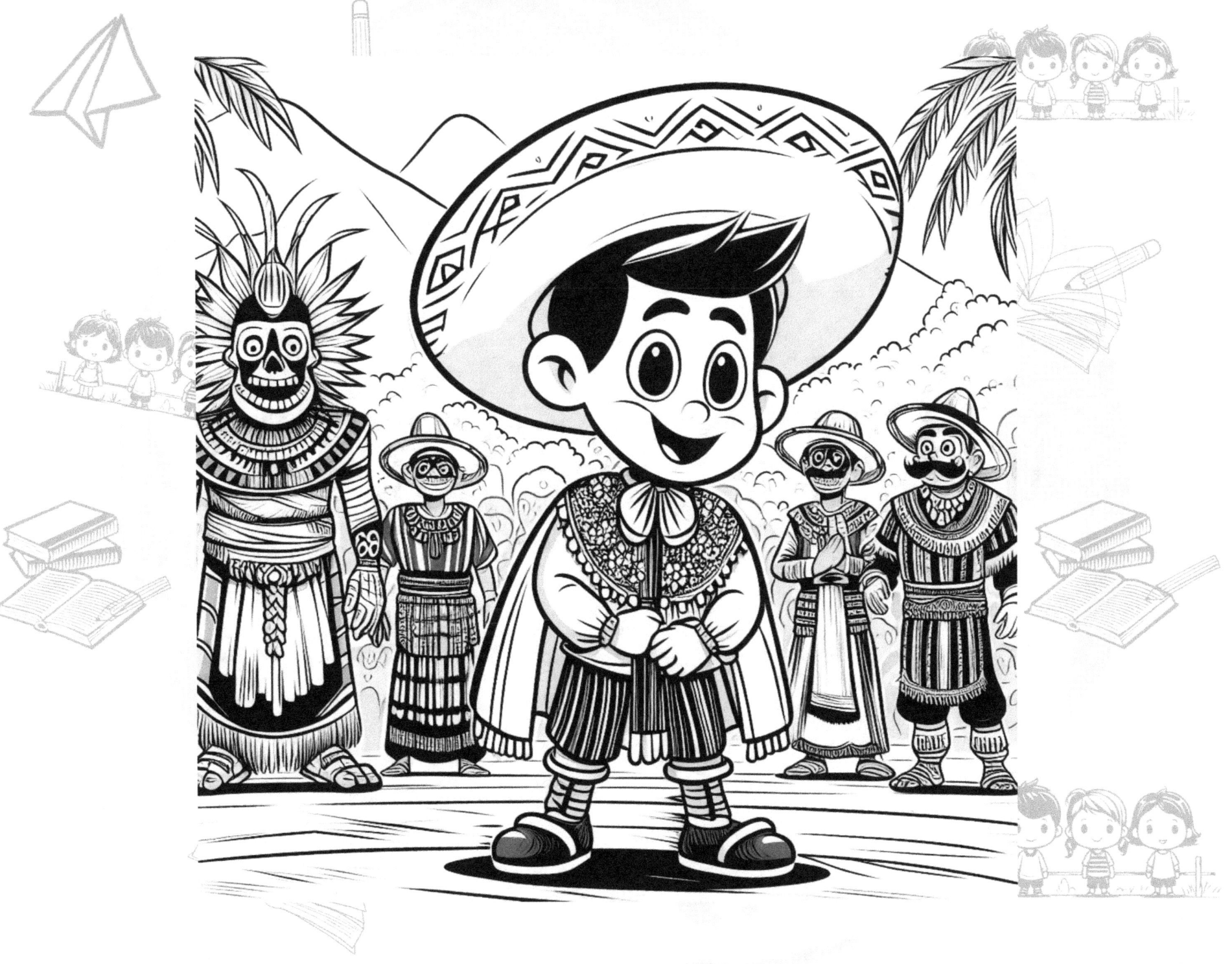

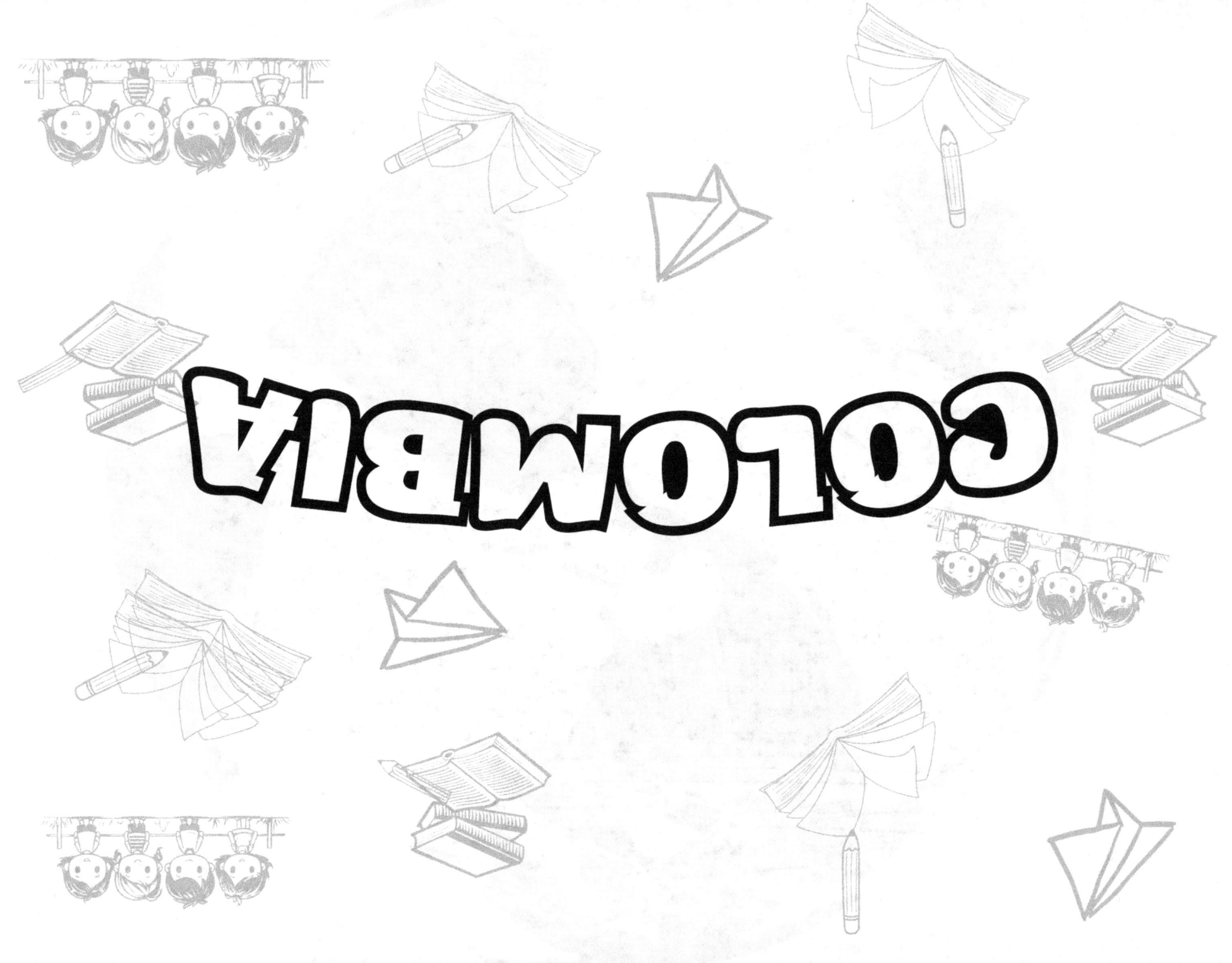

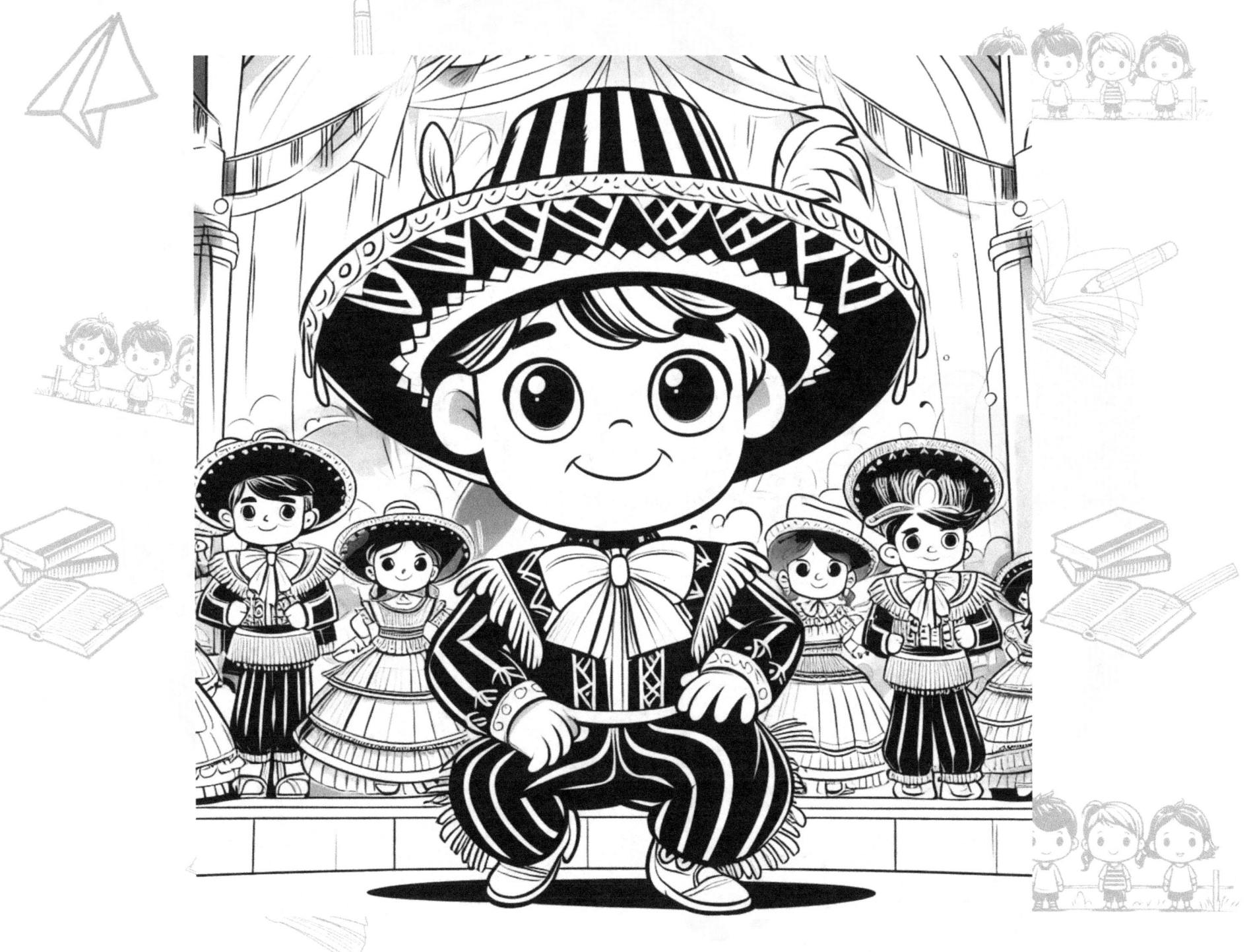

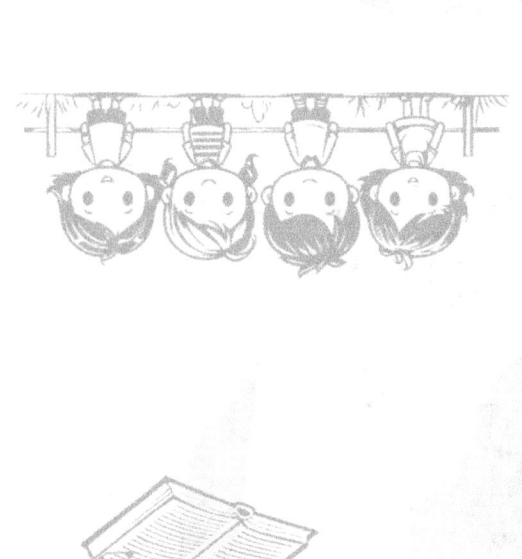
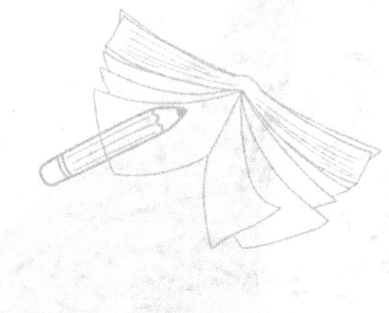

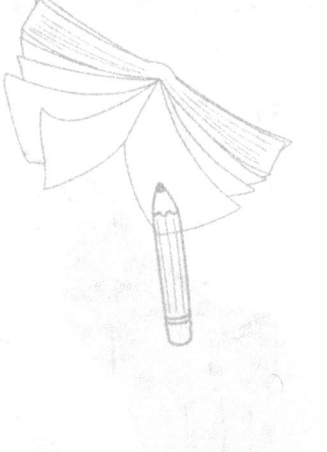
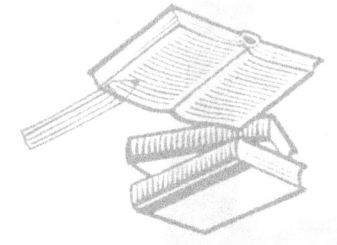
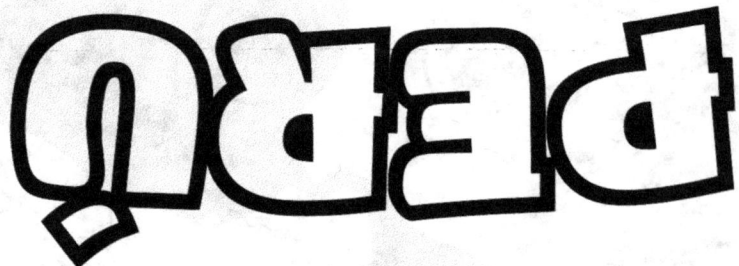
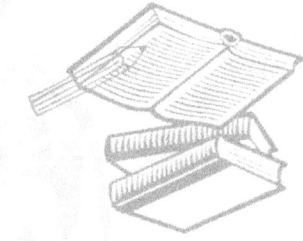
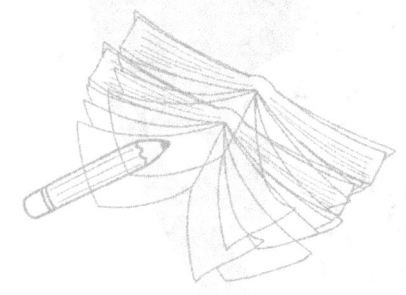
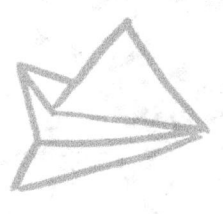
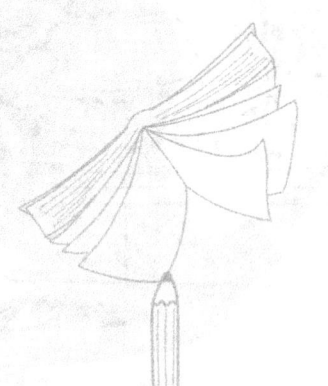
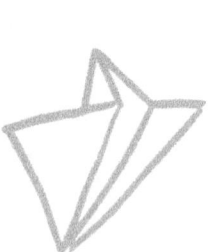
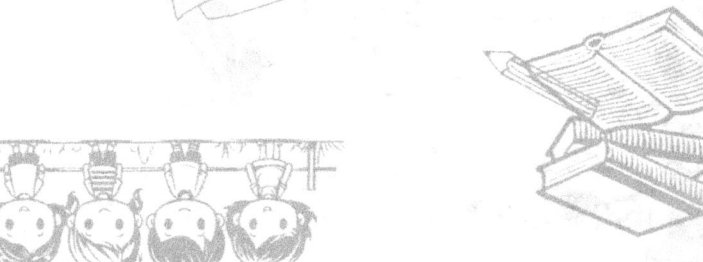

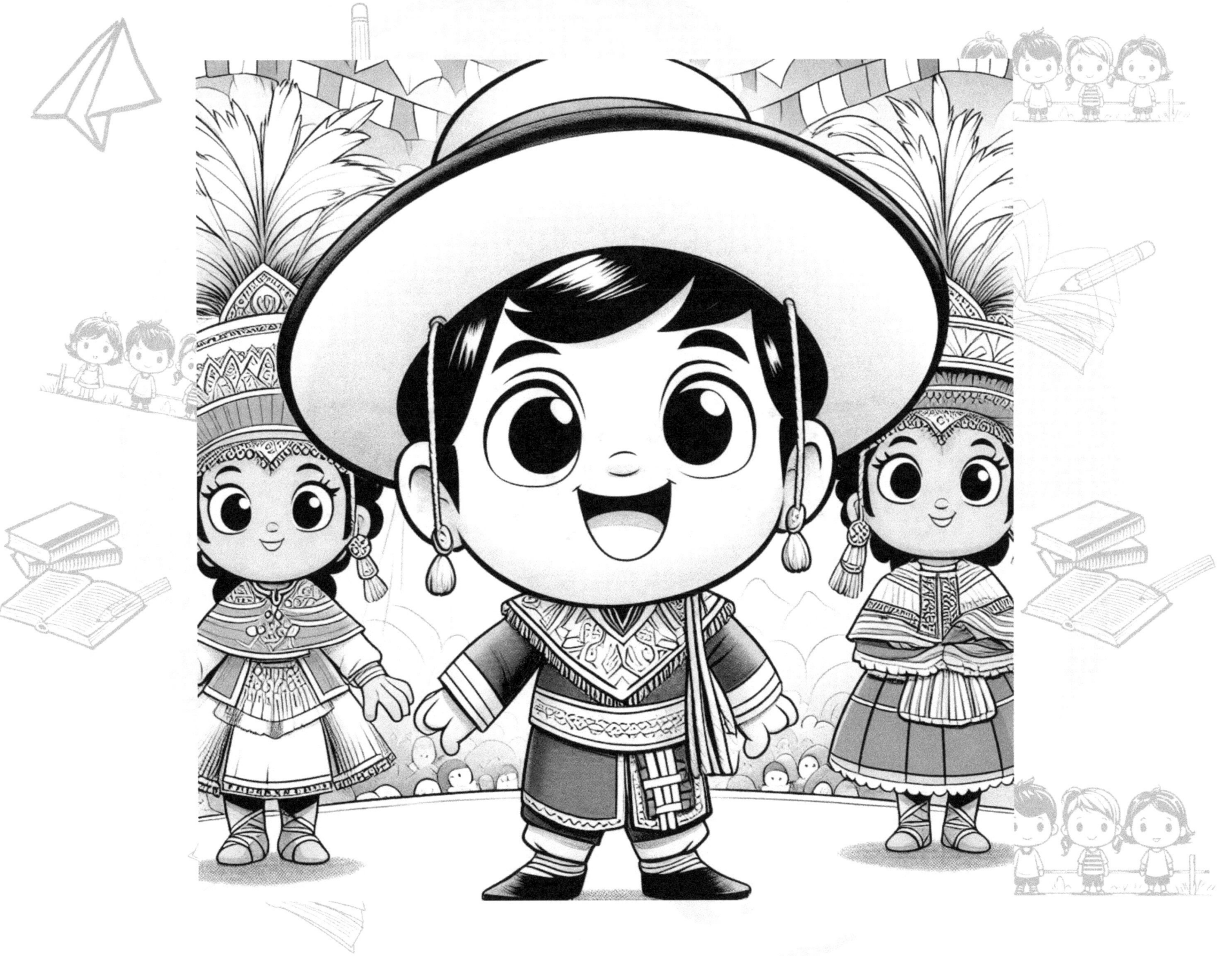

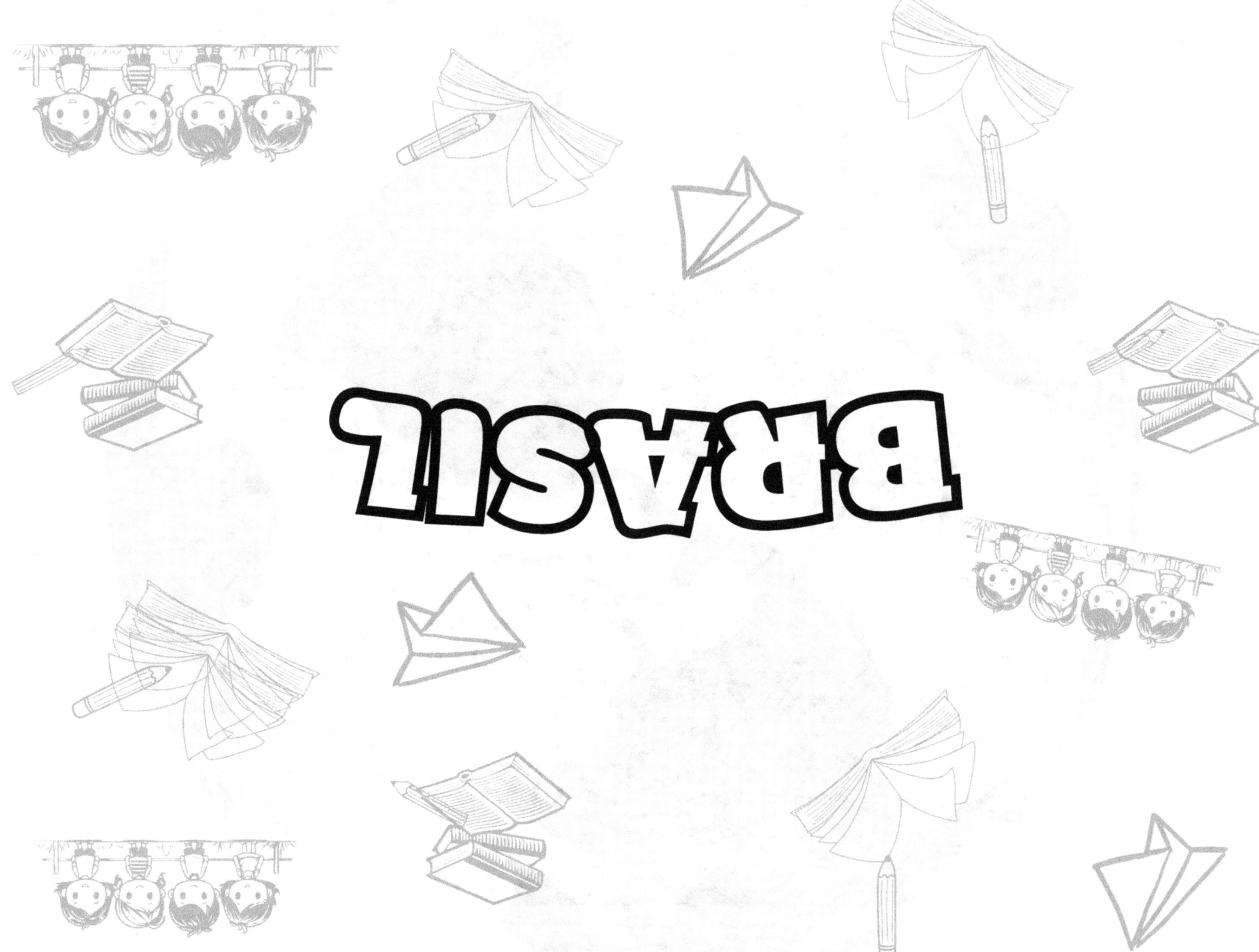

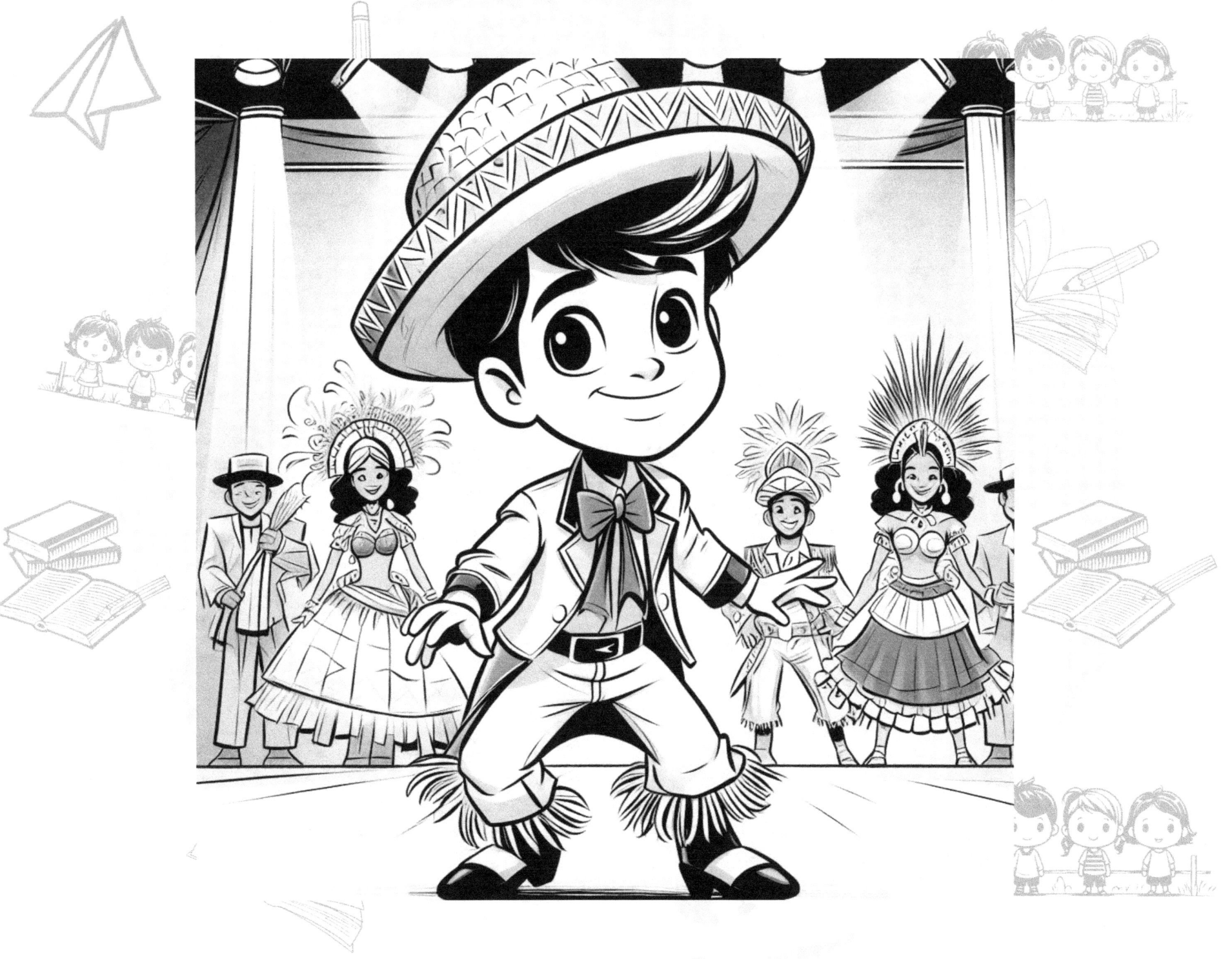

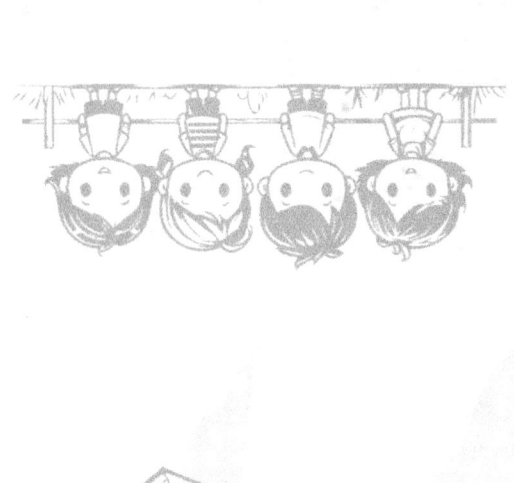
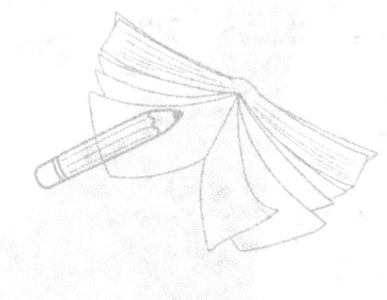
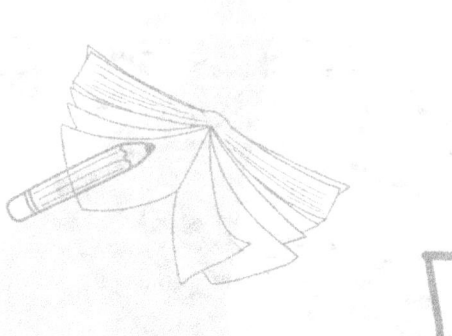
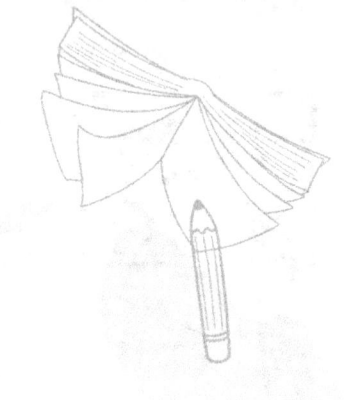
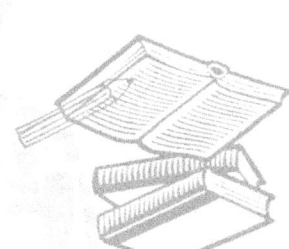
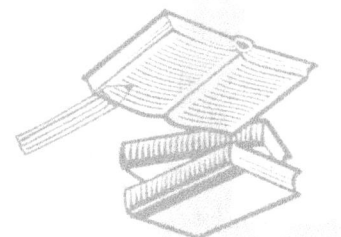

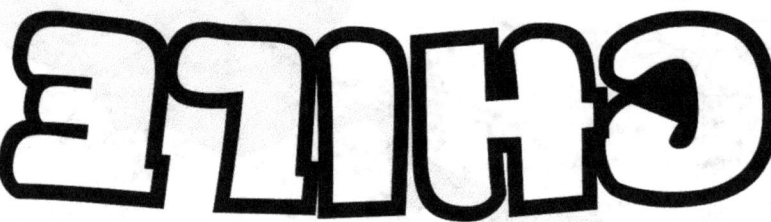
CHILE

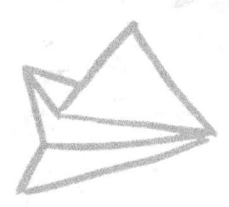
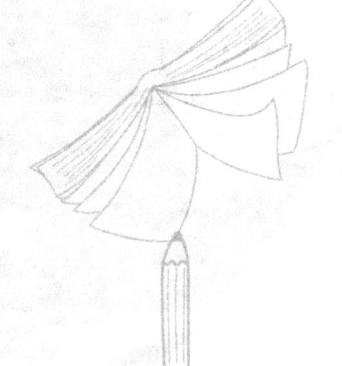
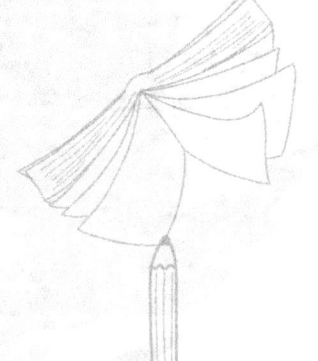
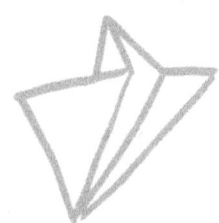

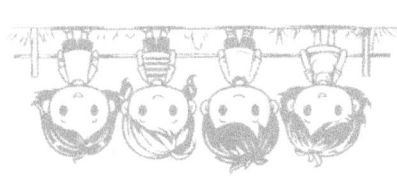

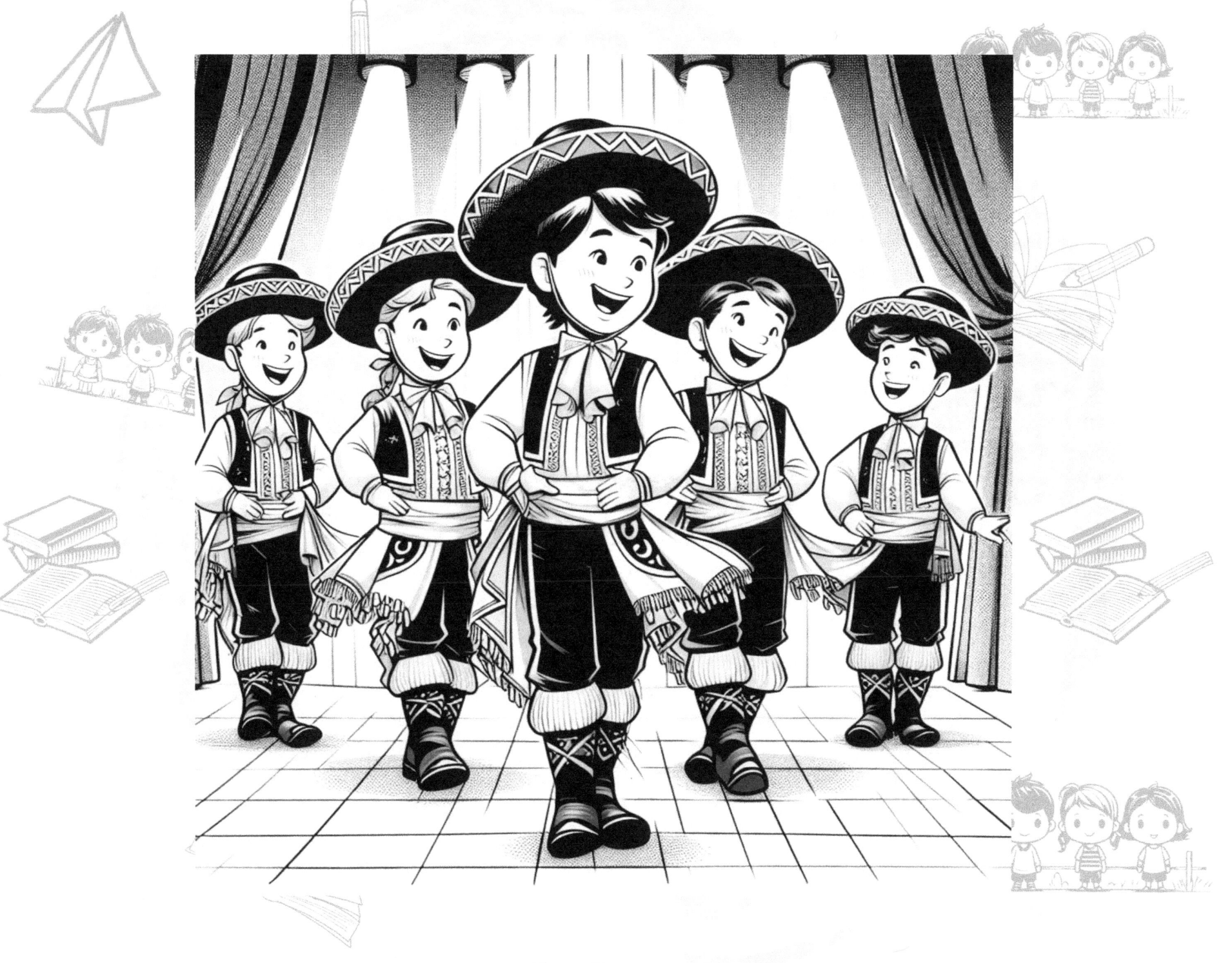

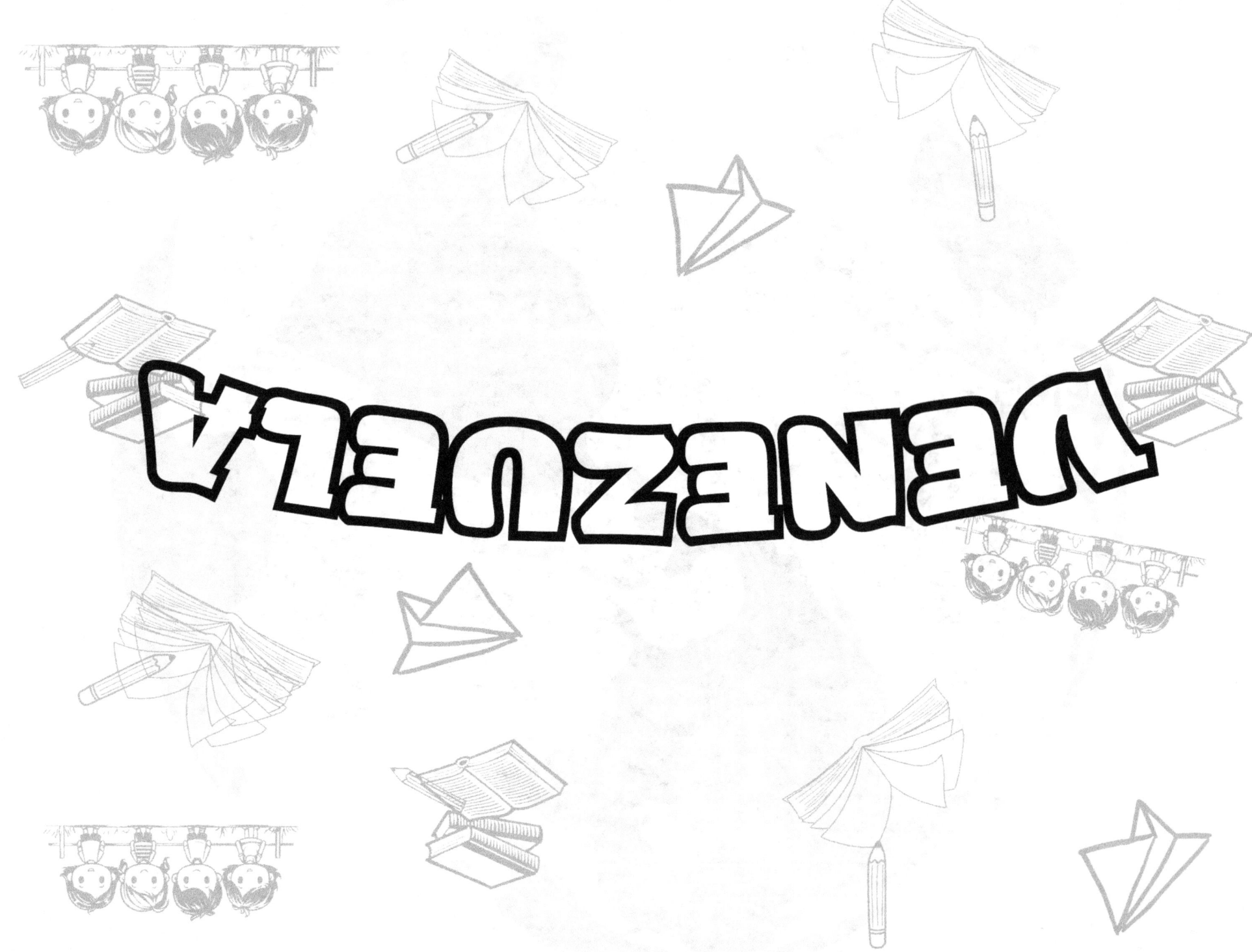

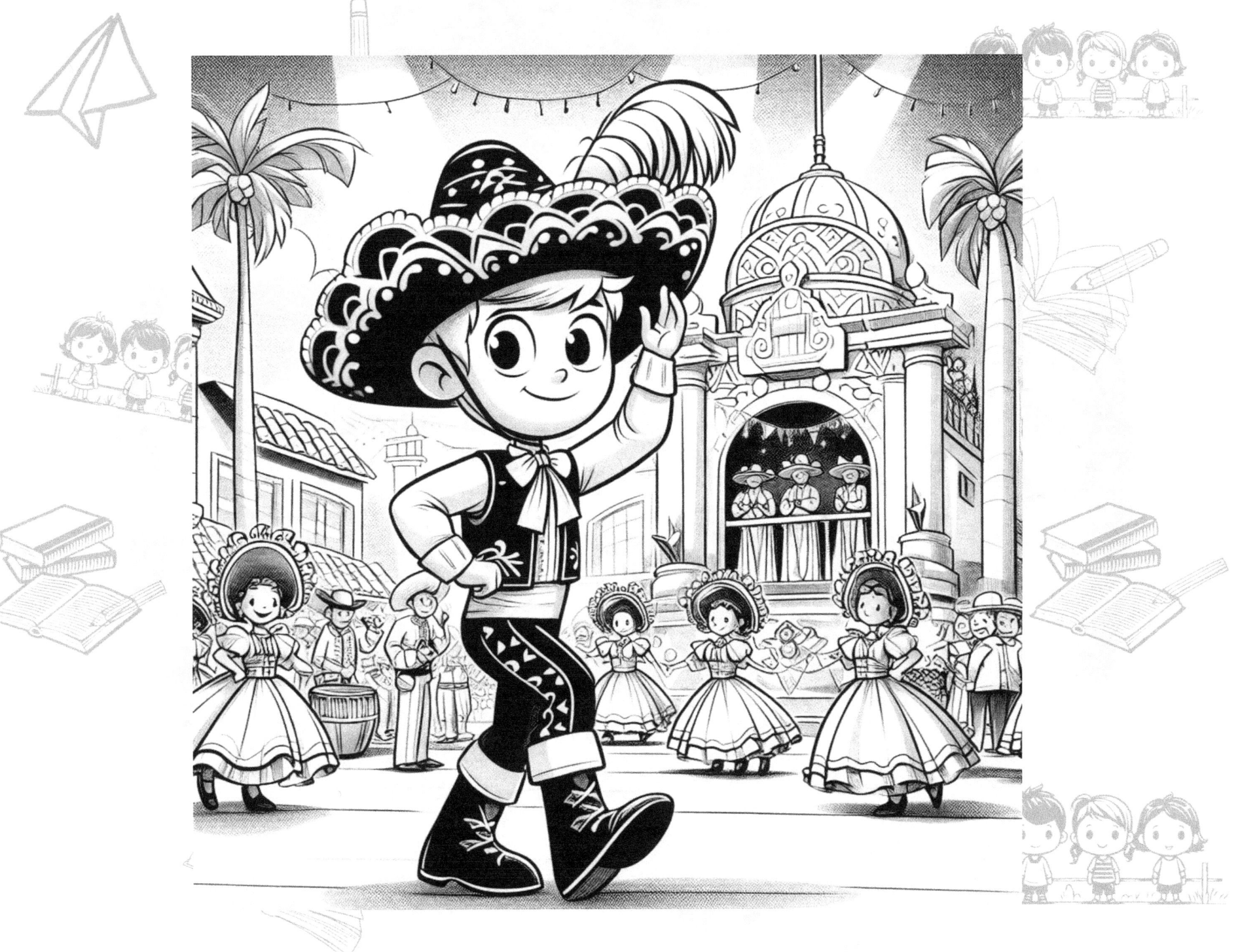

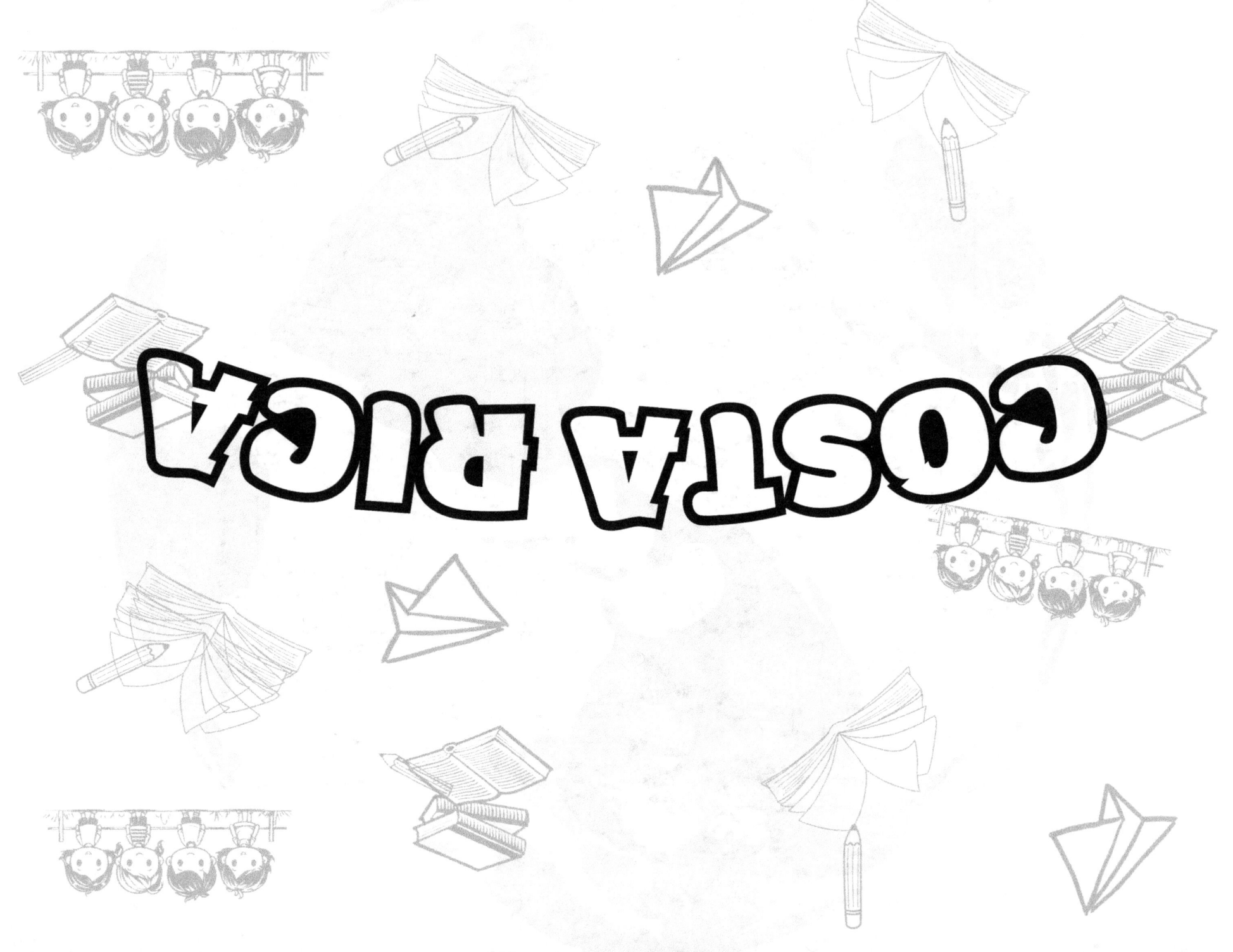

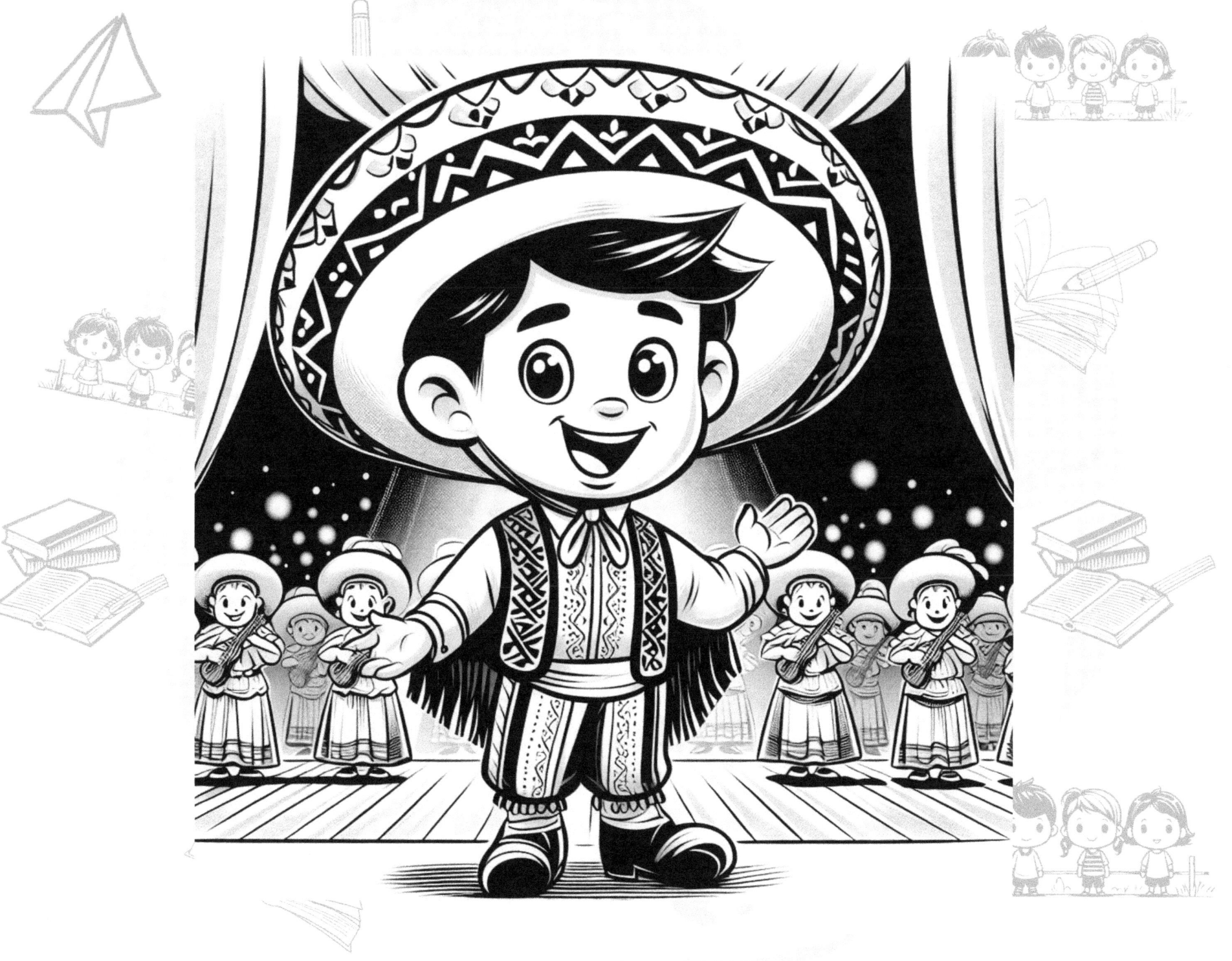

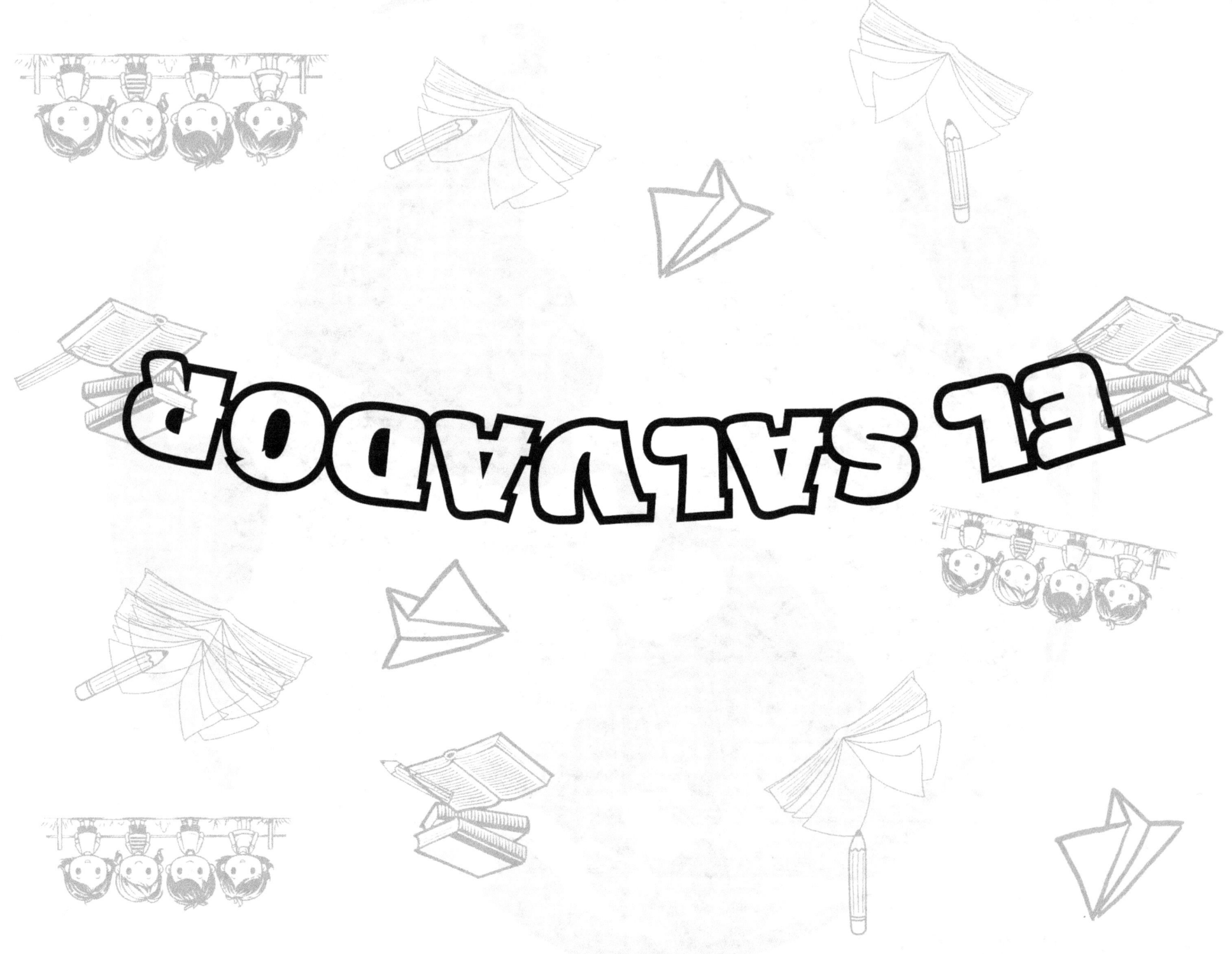

EL SALVADOR

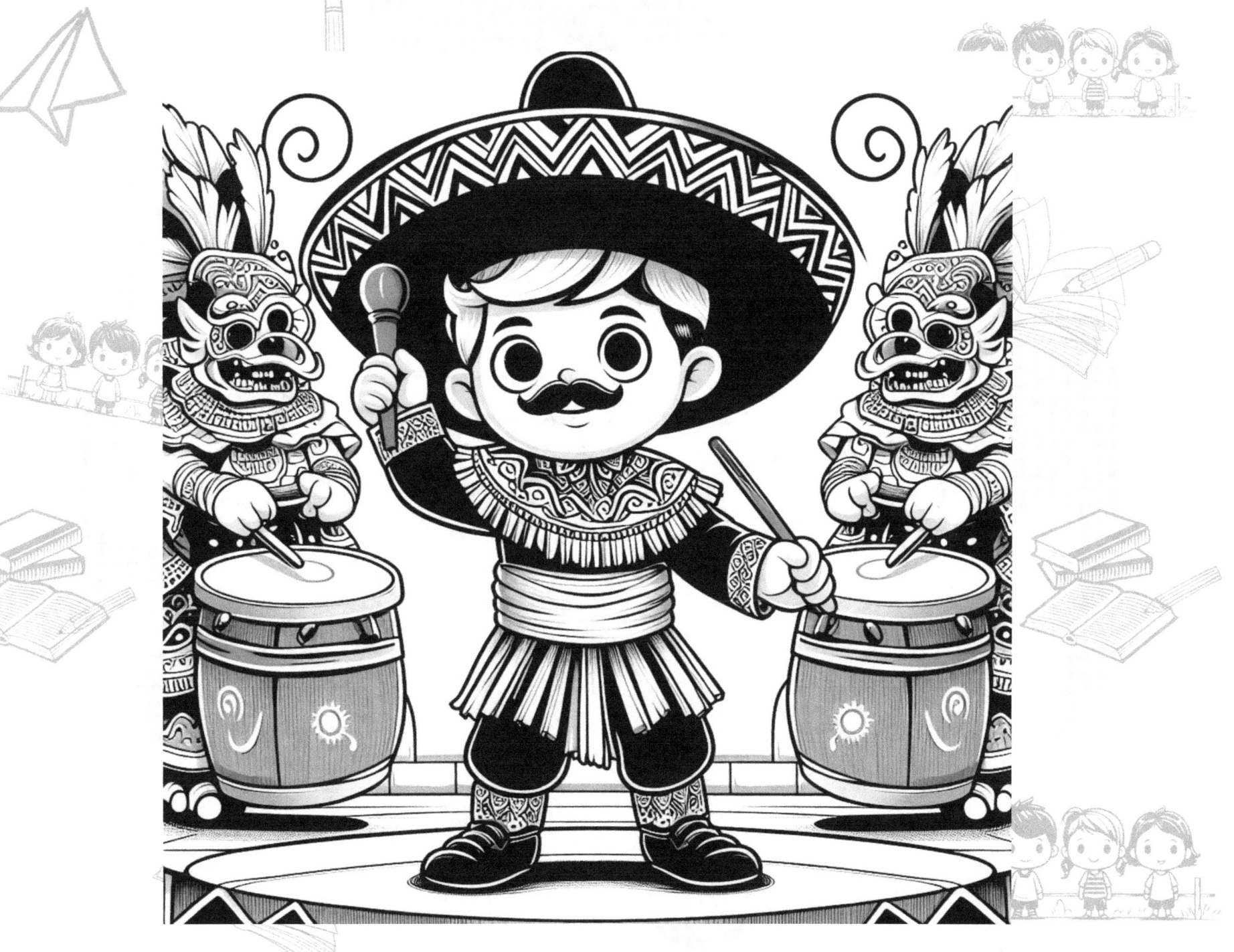

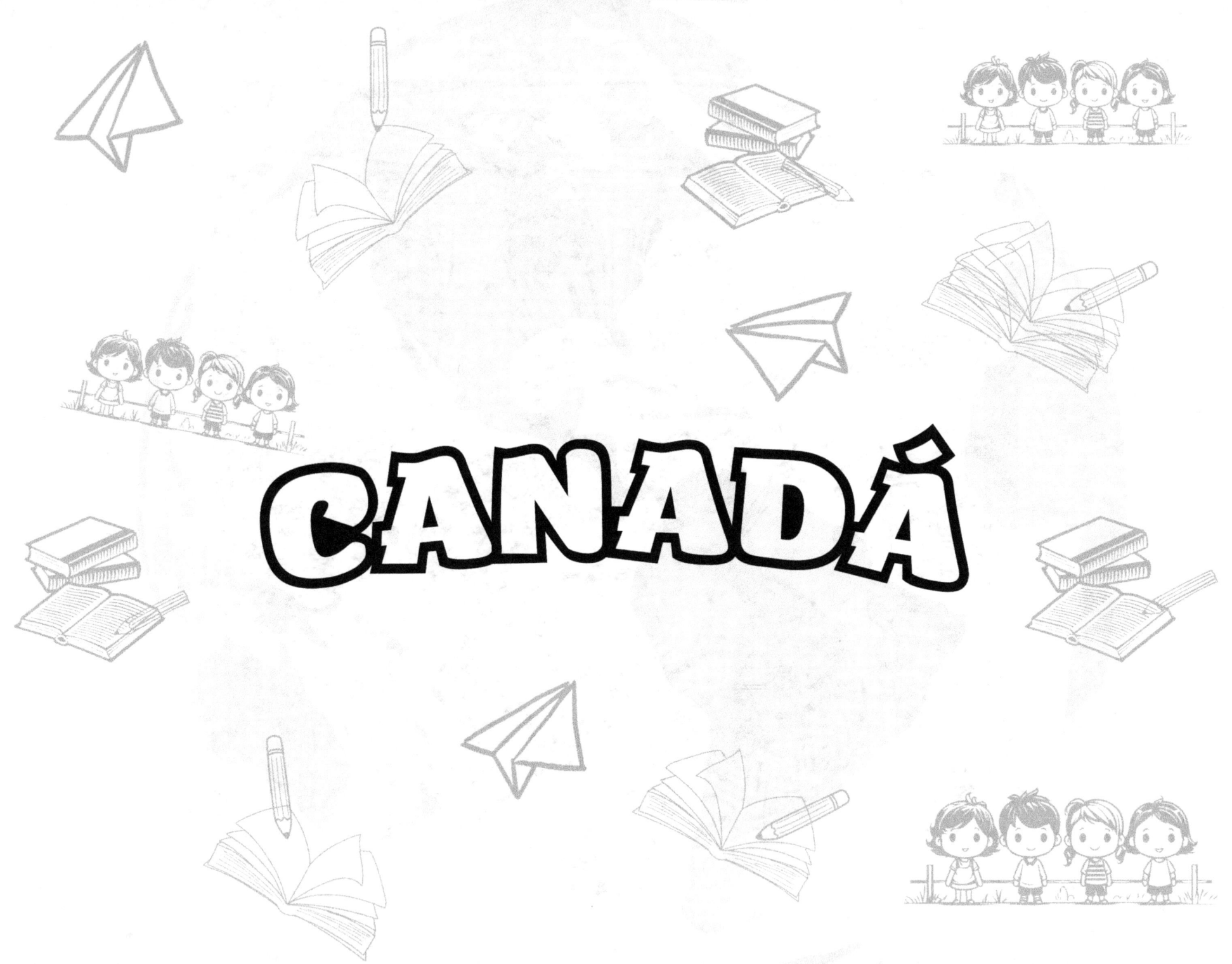

CANADÁ

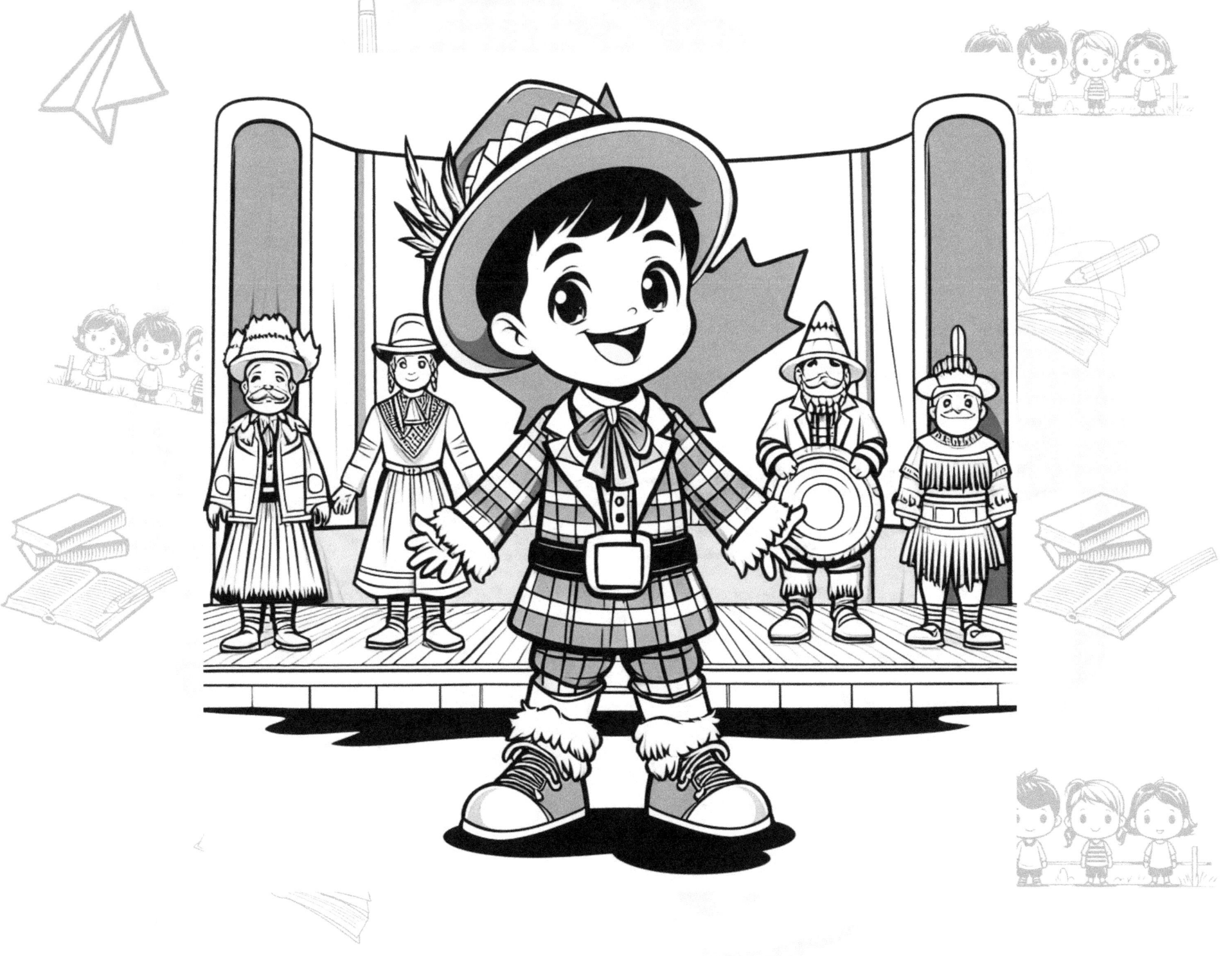

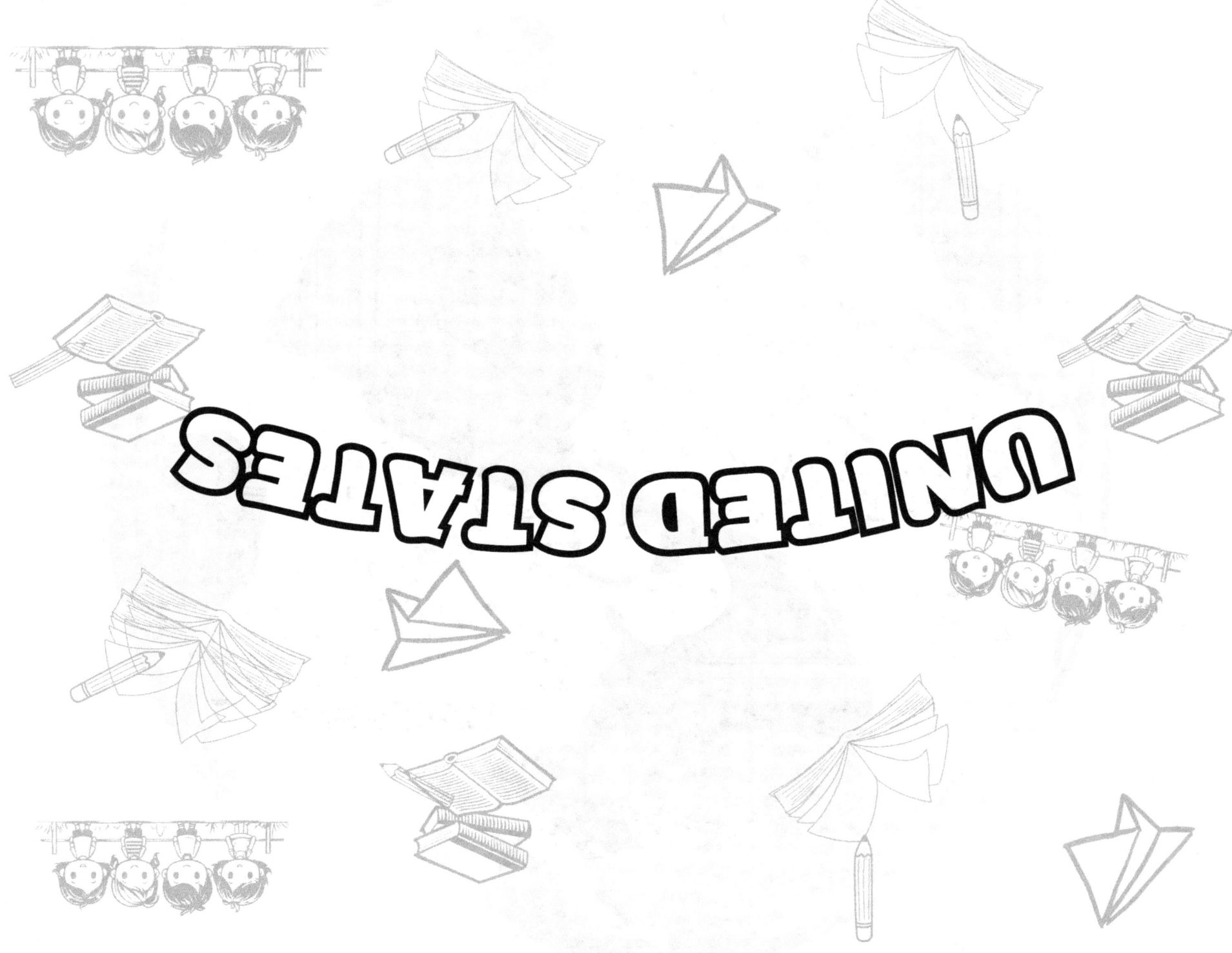

UNITED STATES

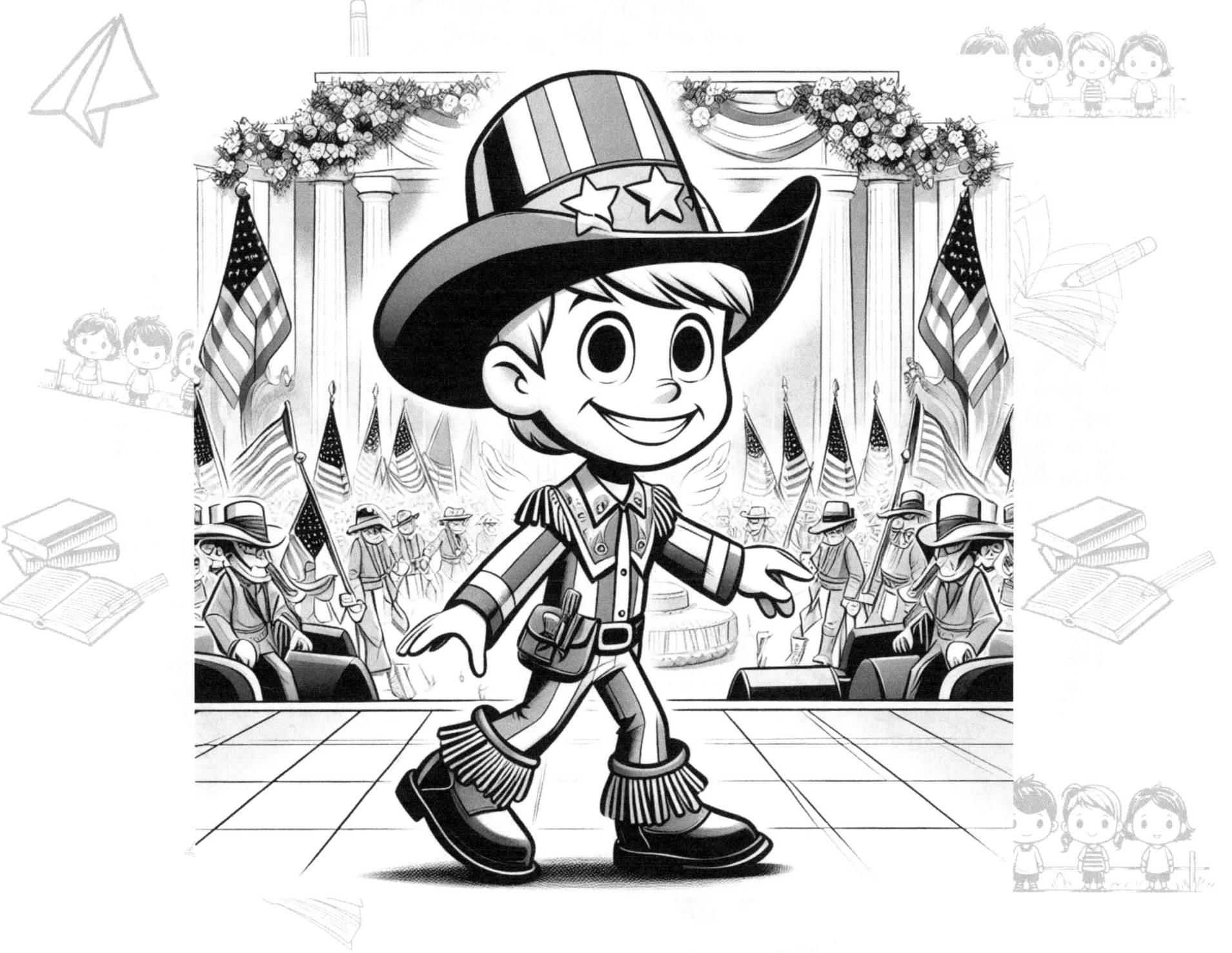

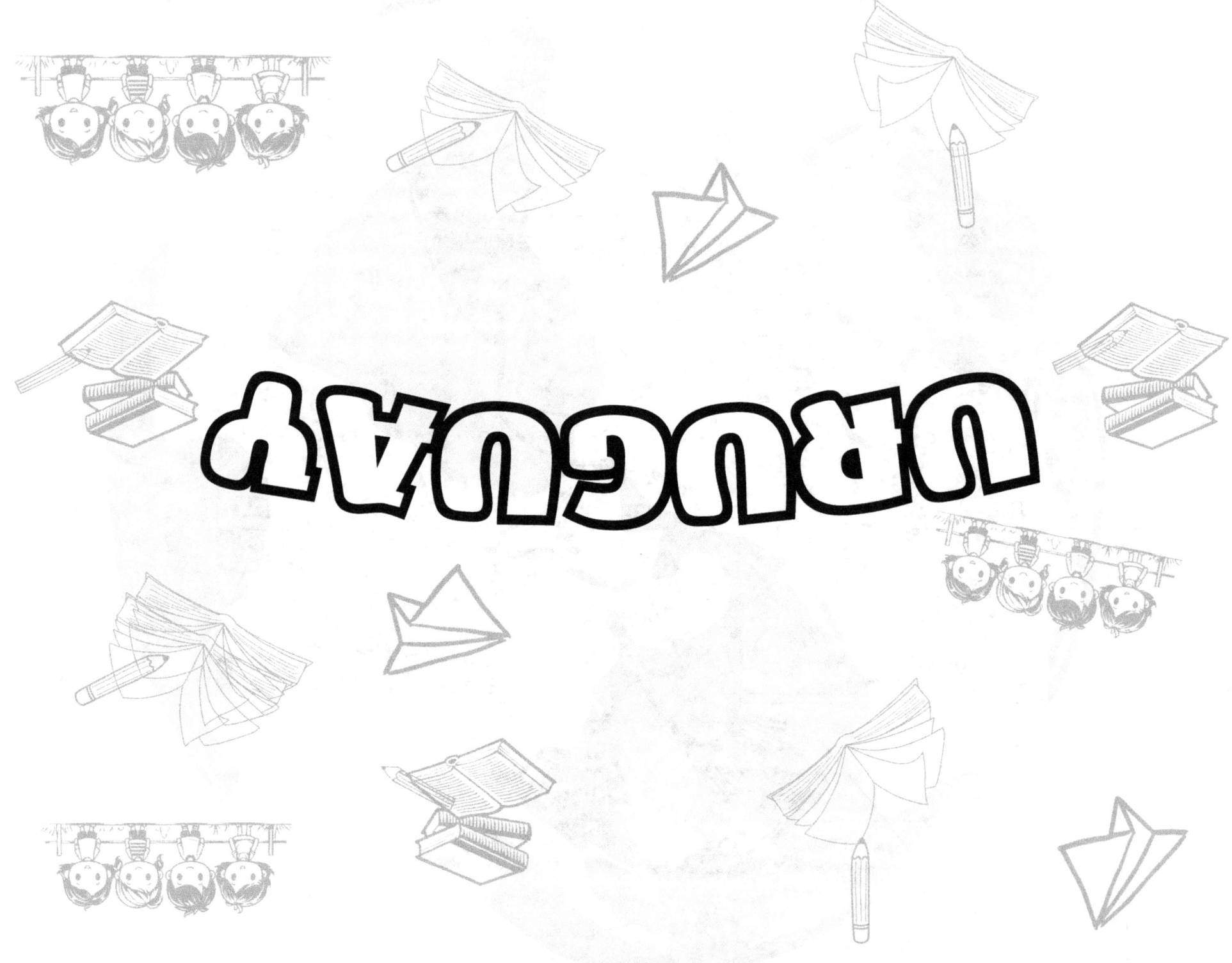

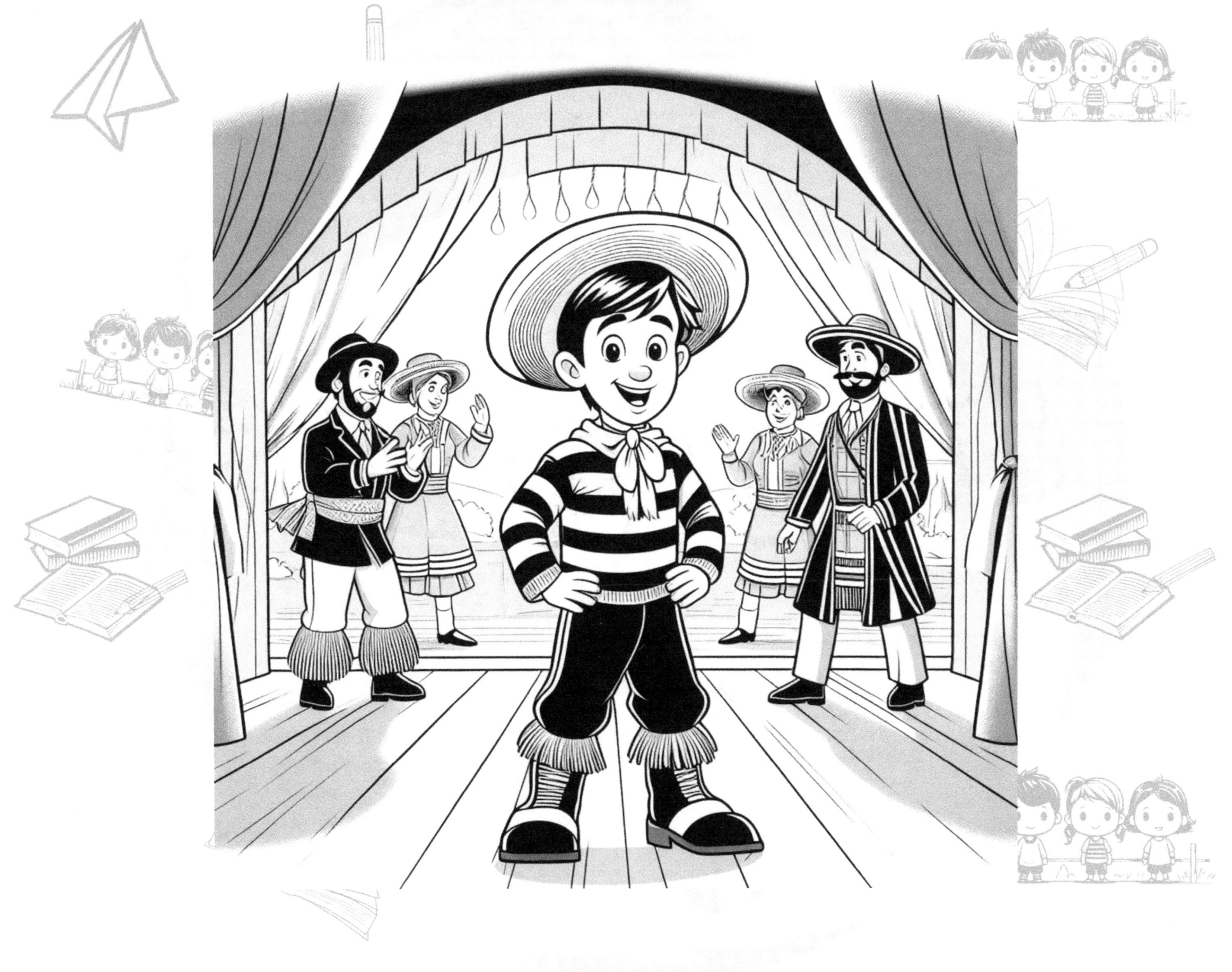

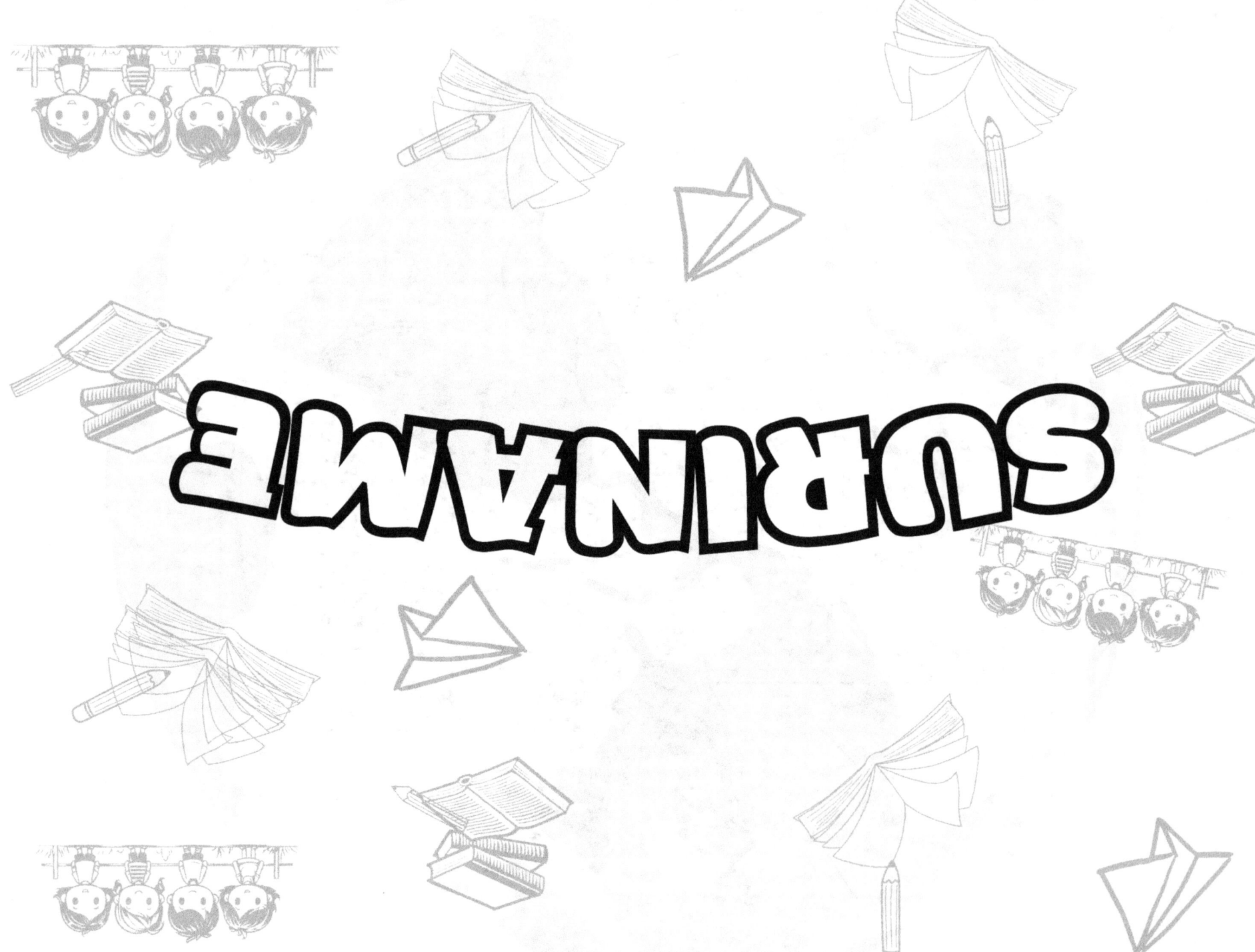

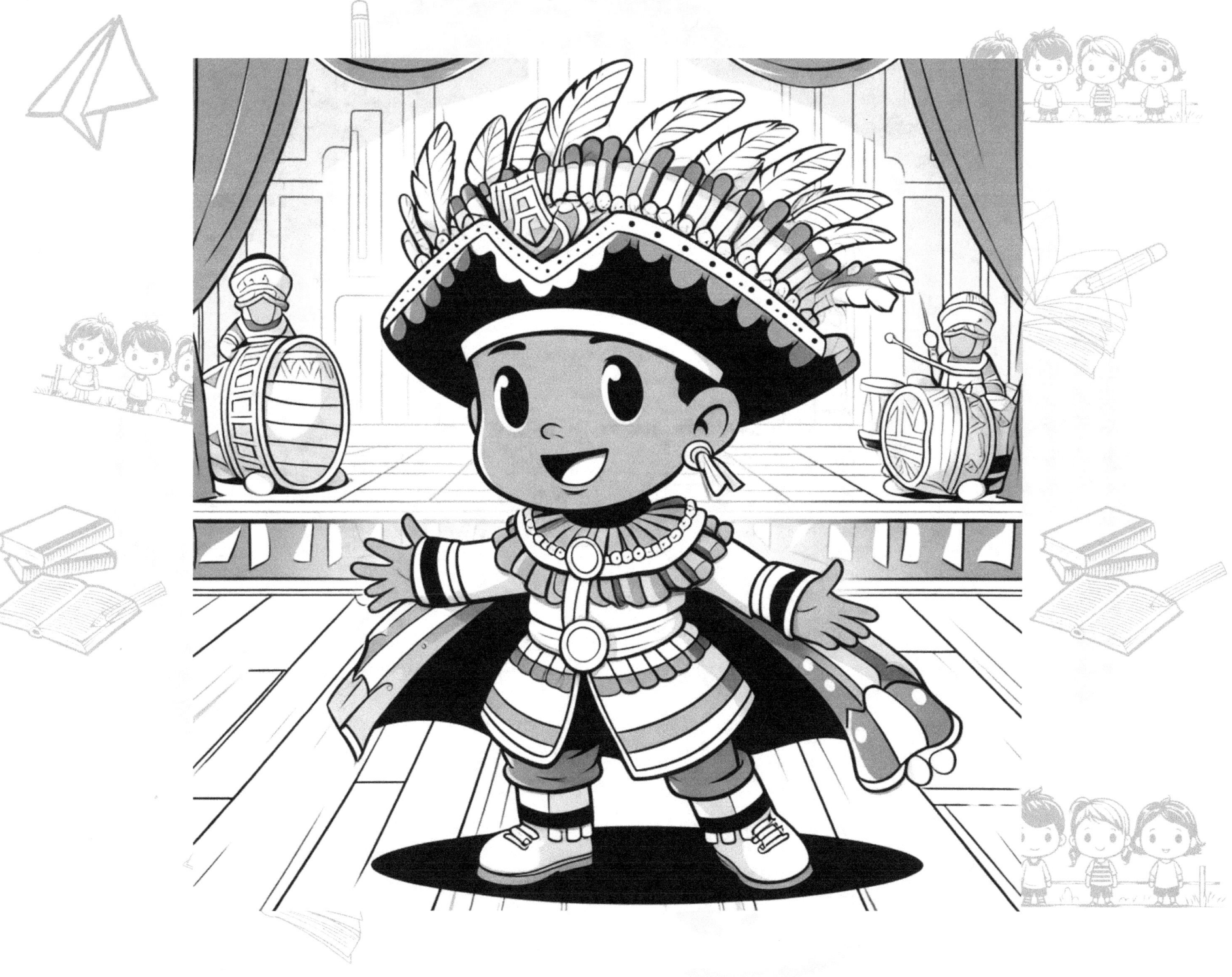

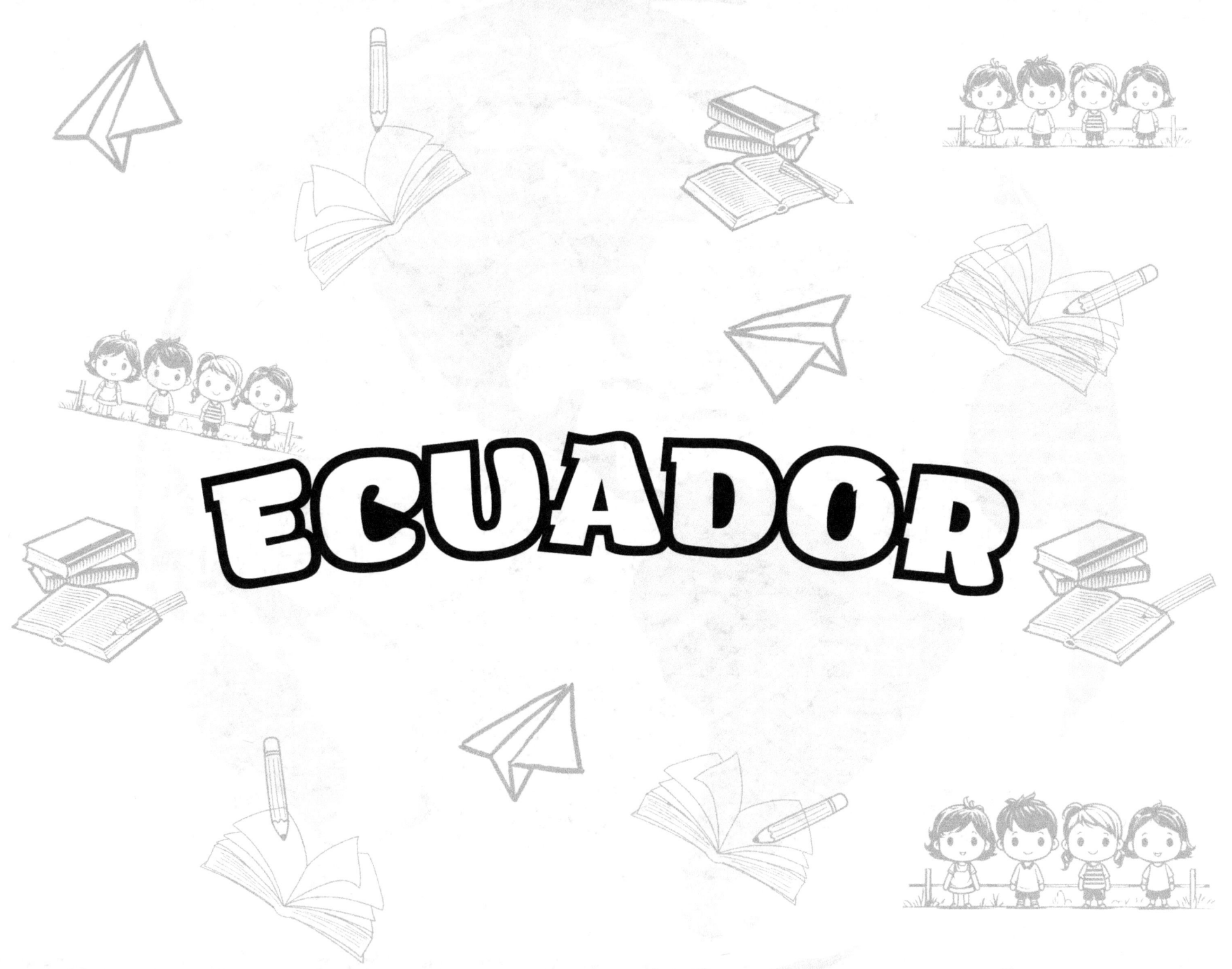

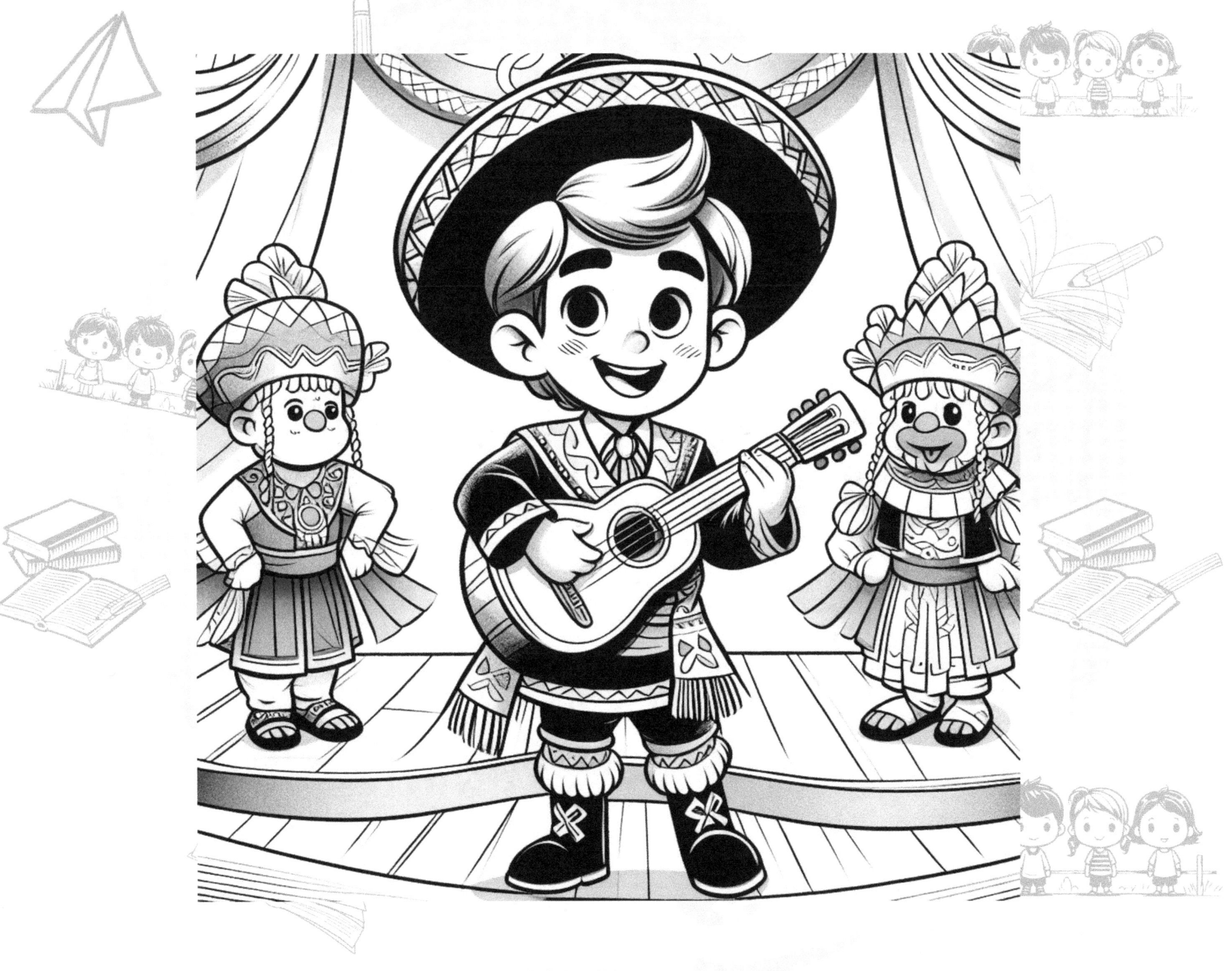

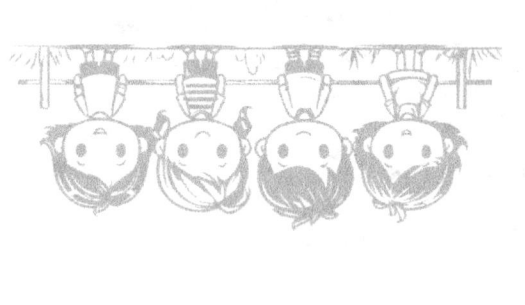
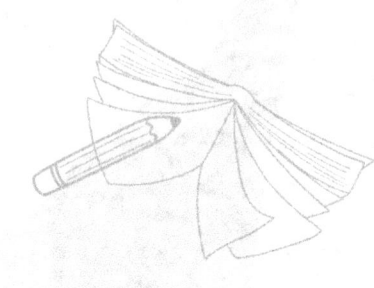
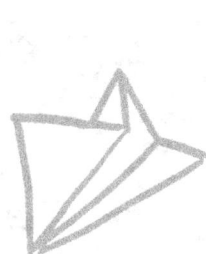
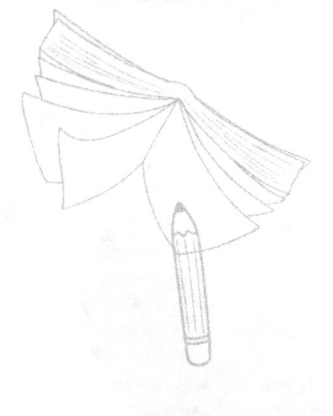
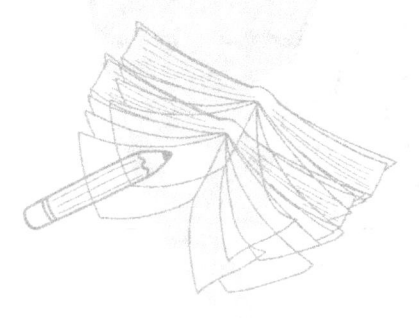

ARGENTINA

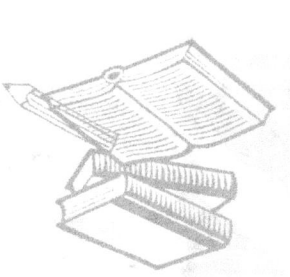
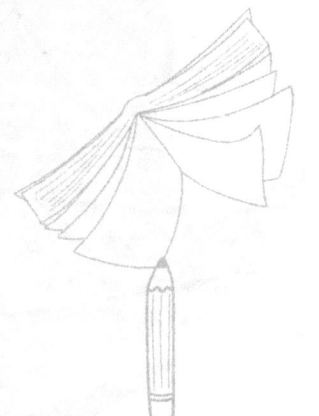
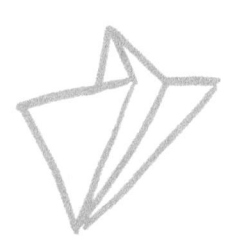
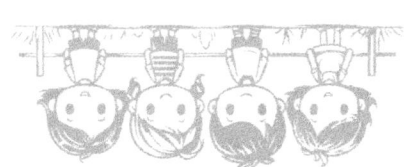

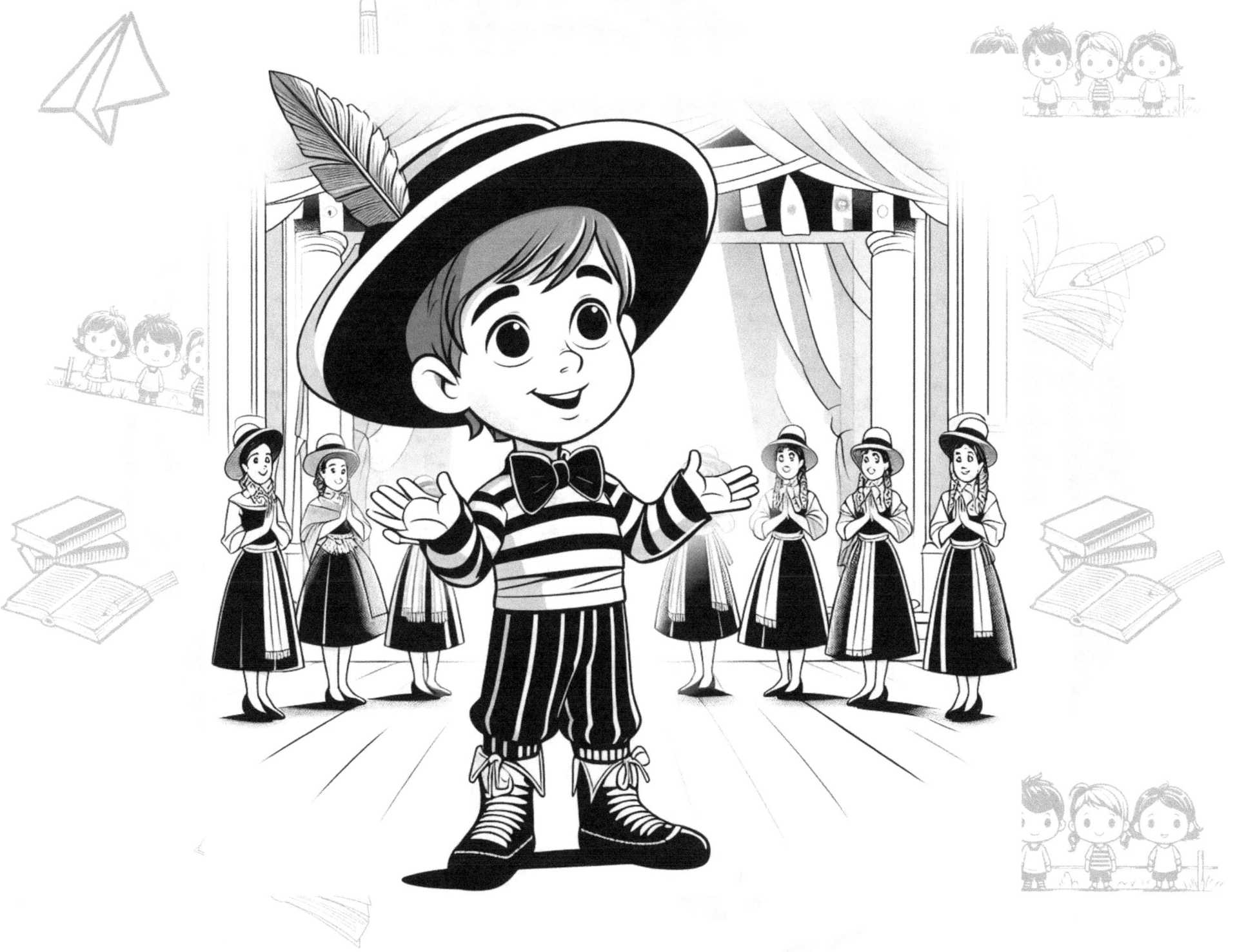

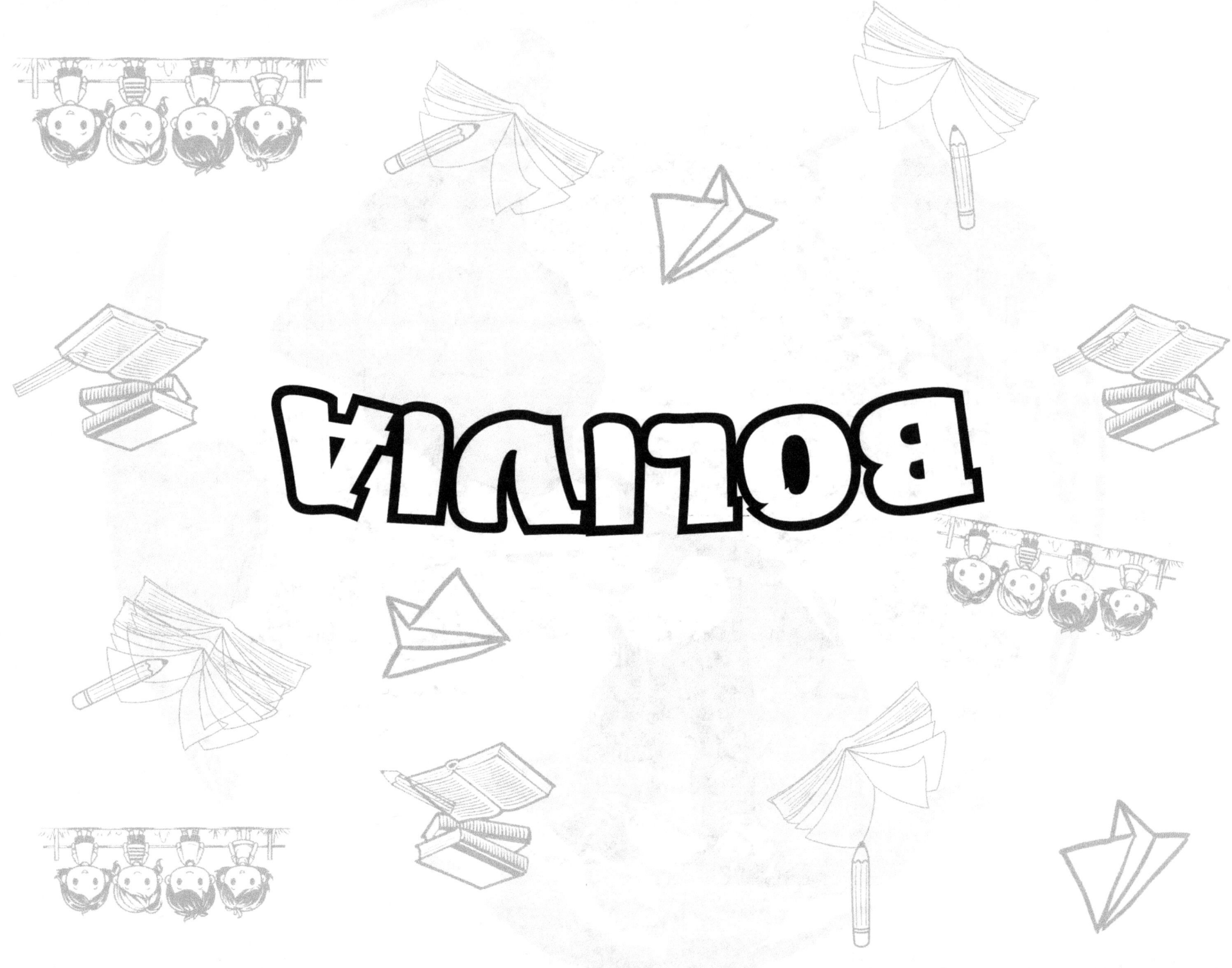

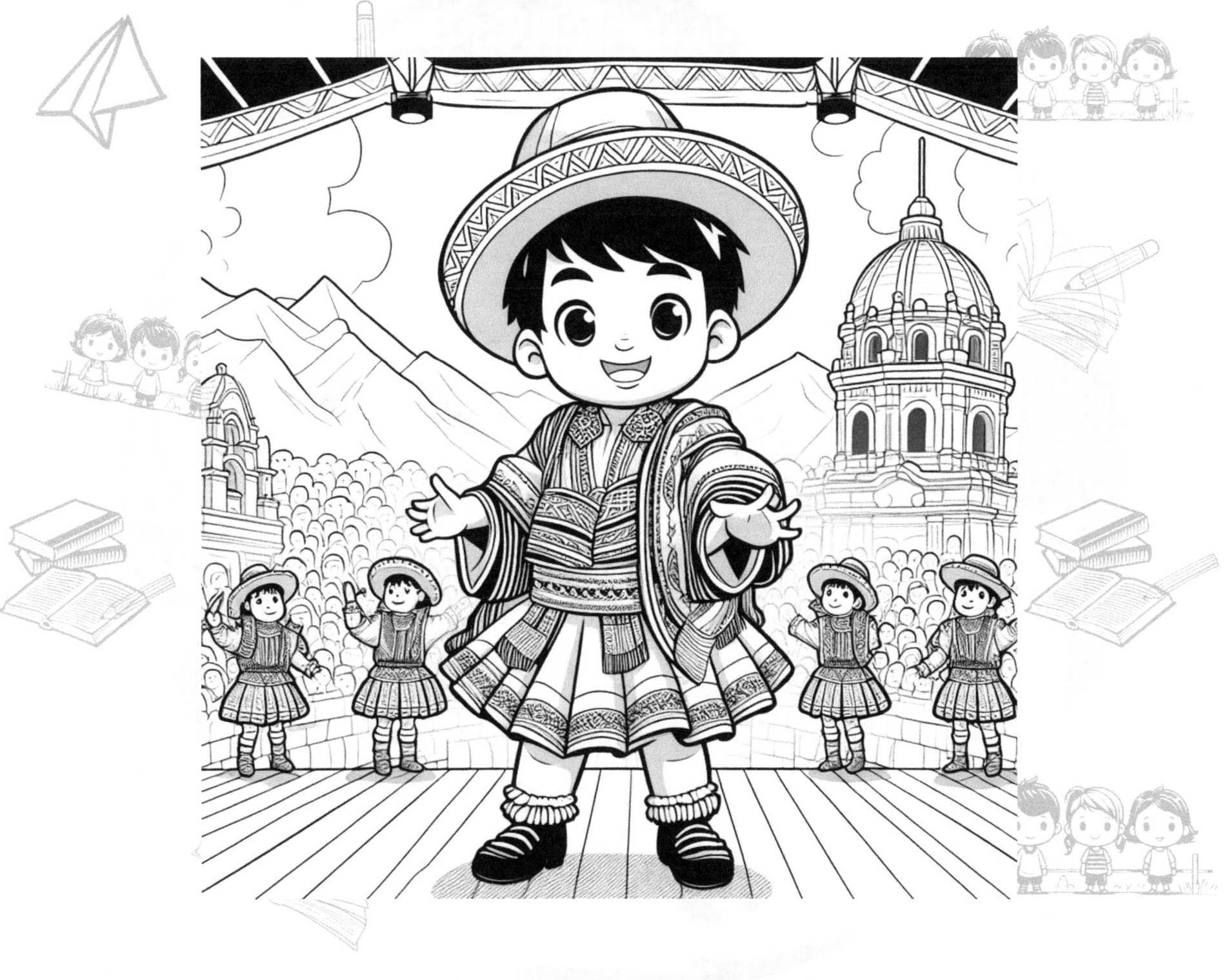

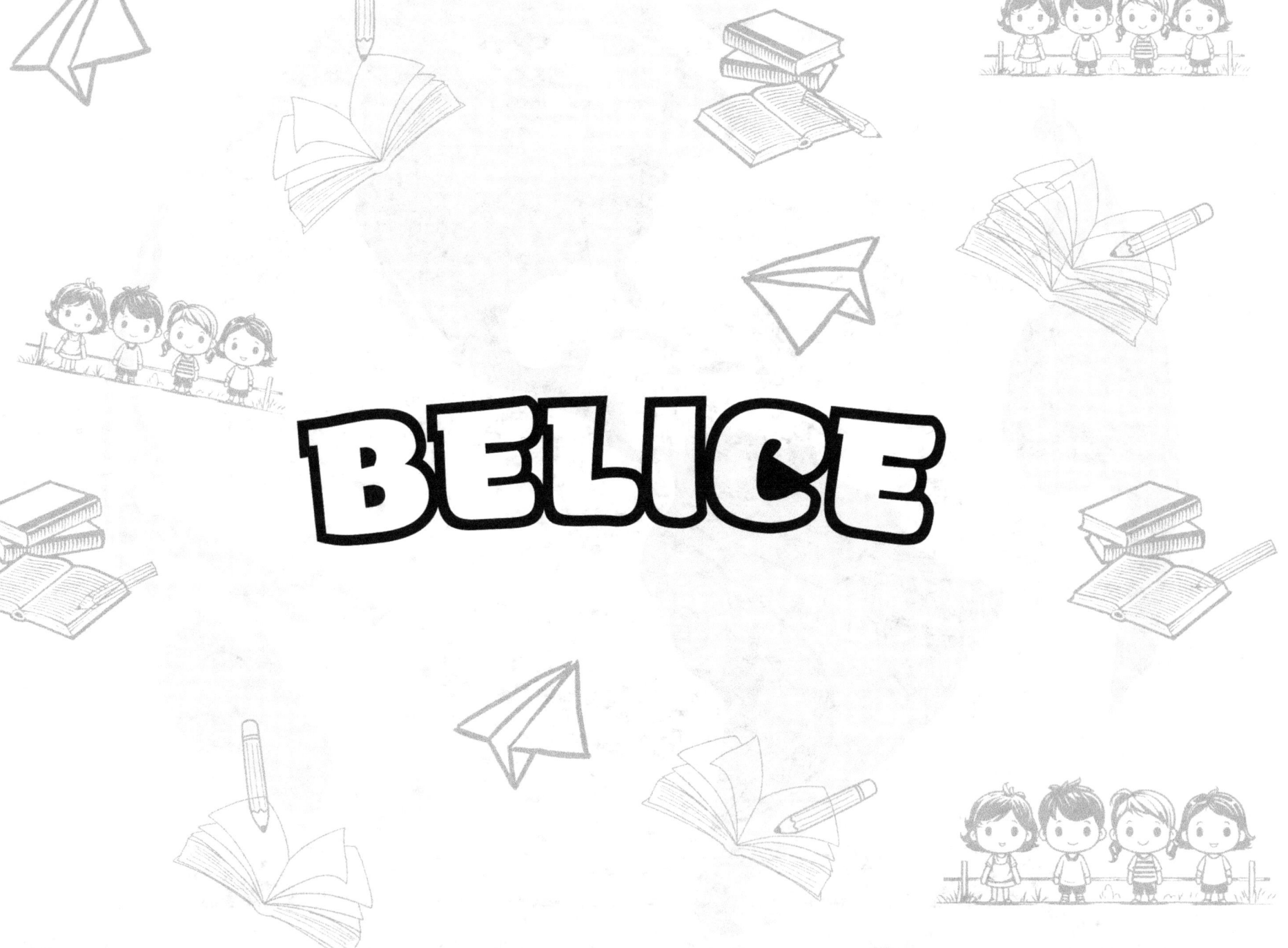

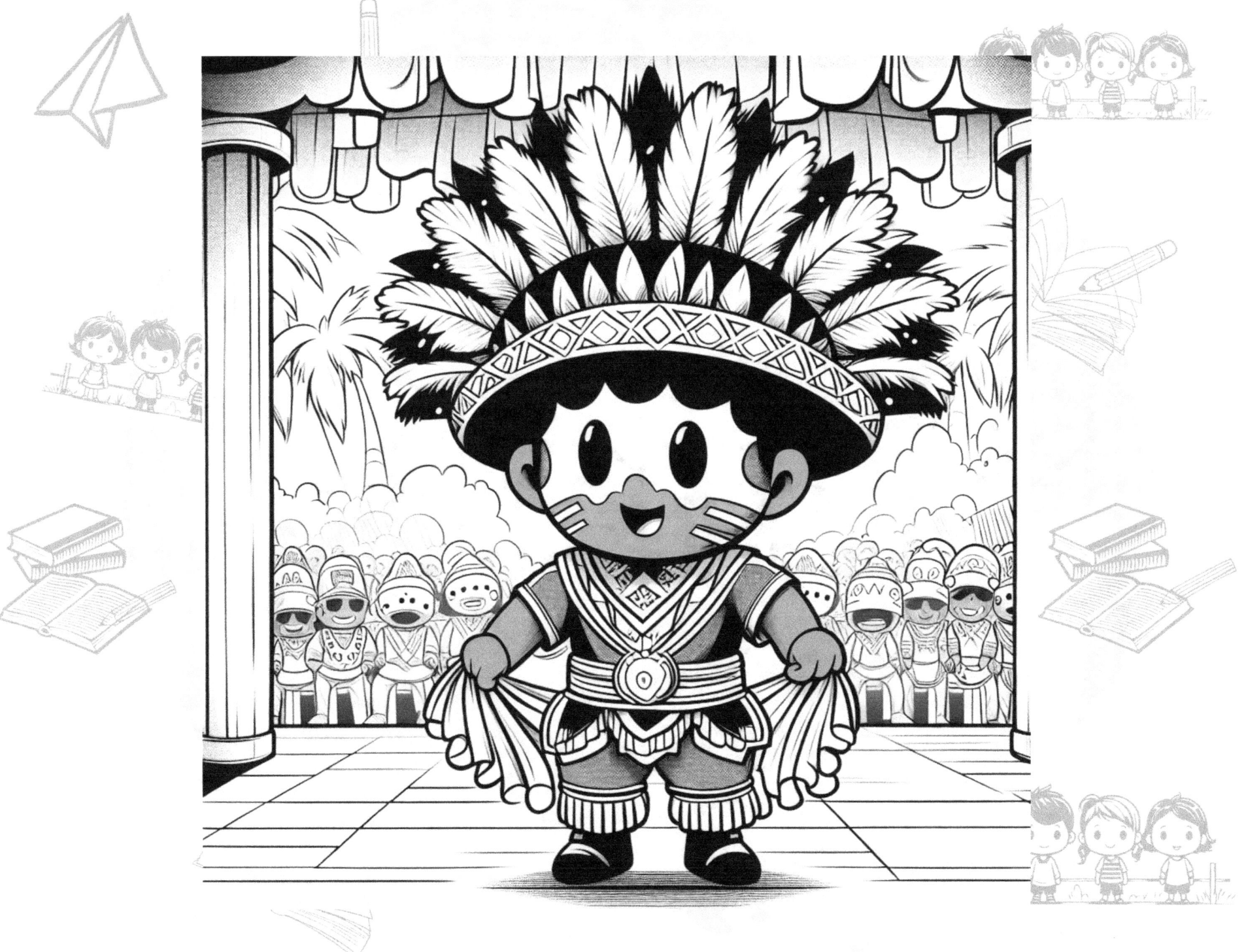

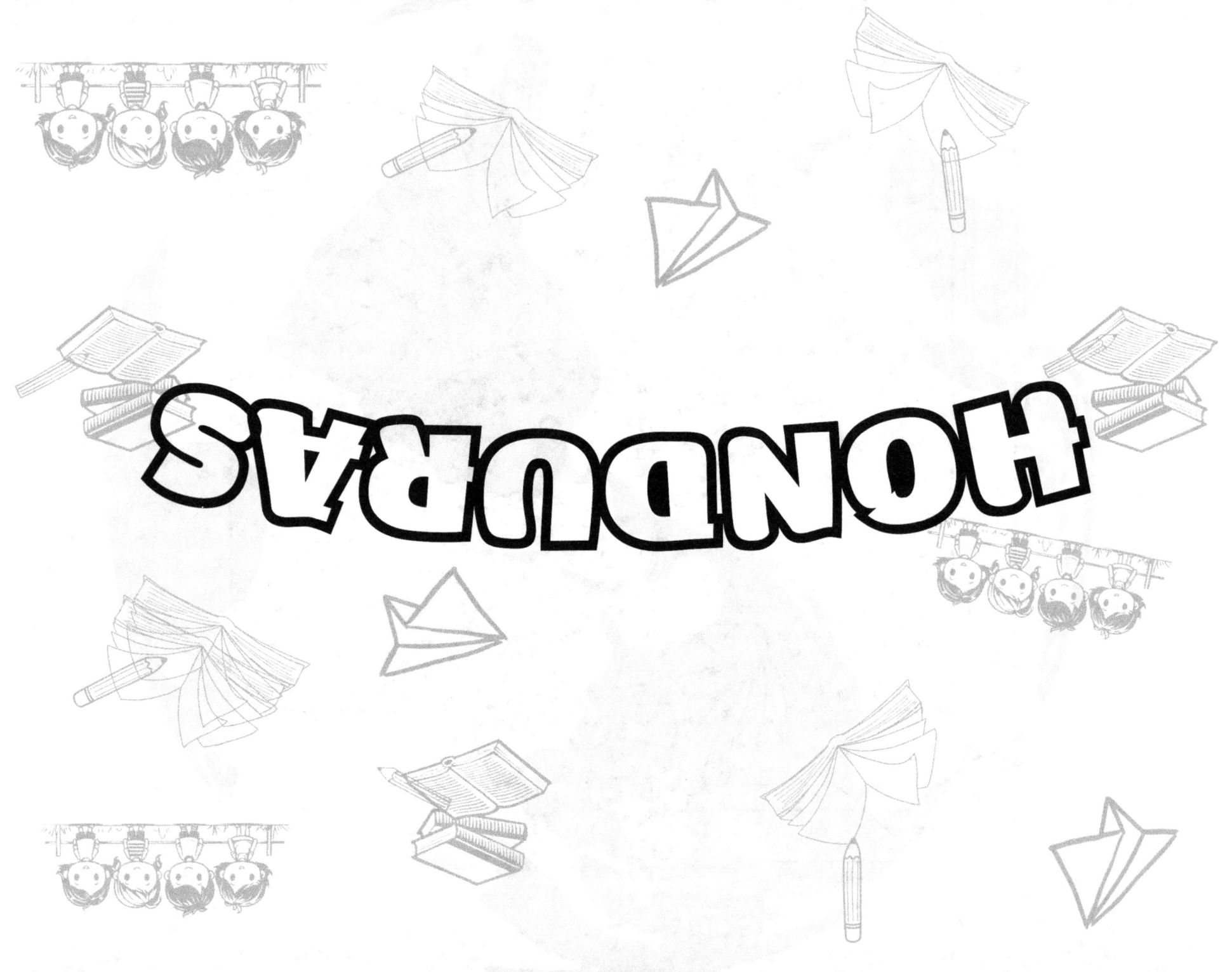

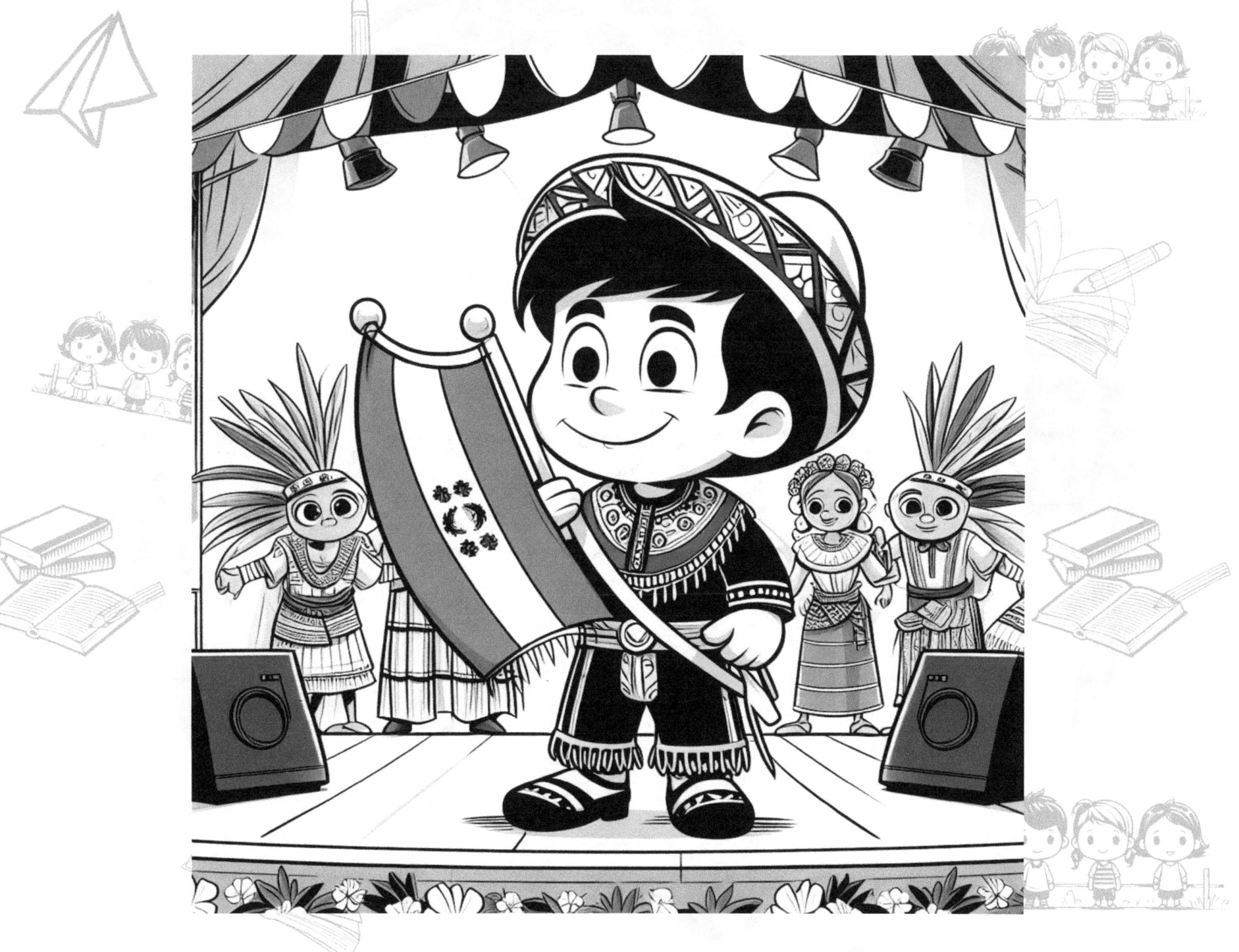

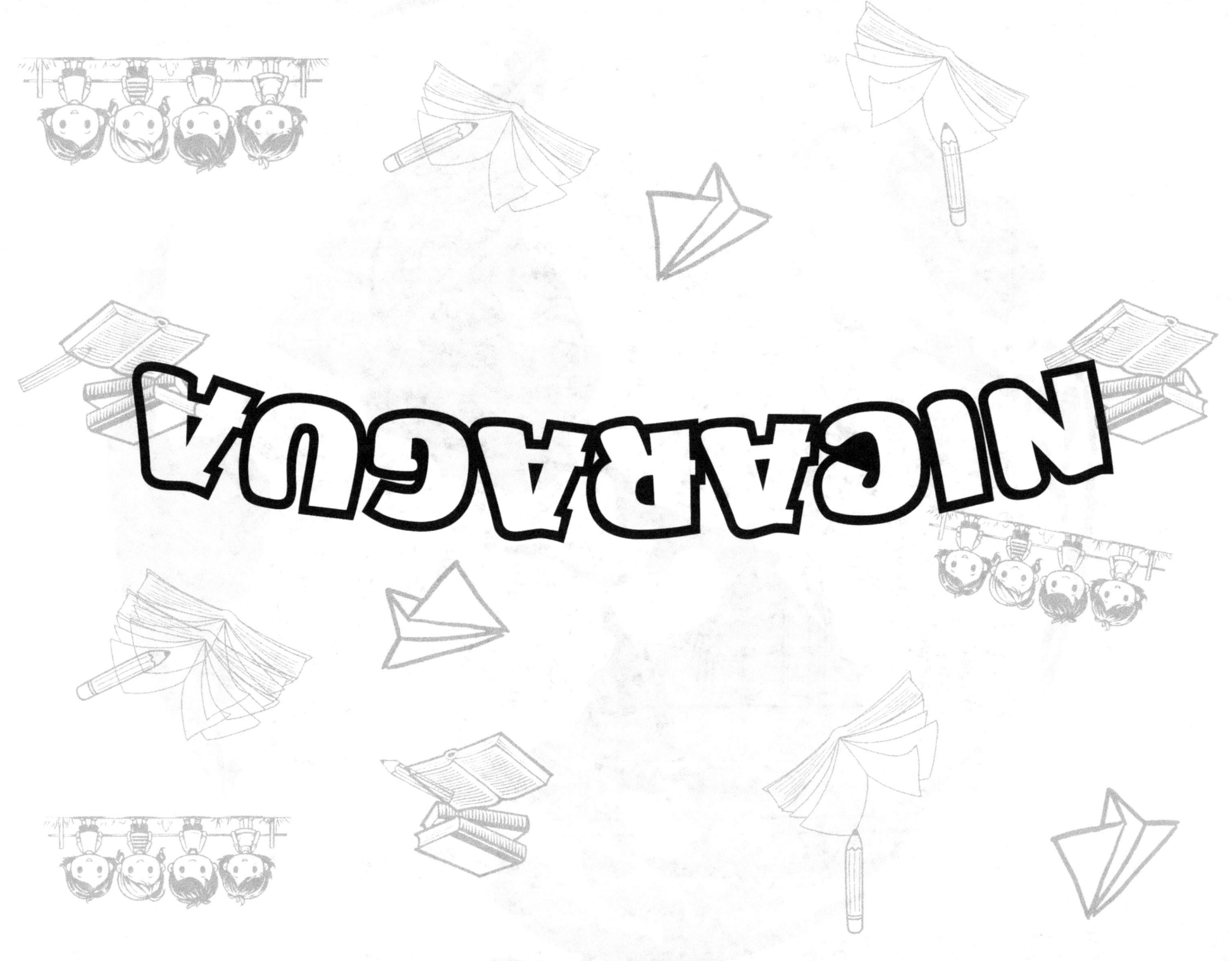

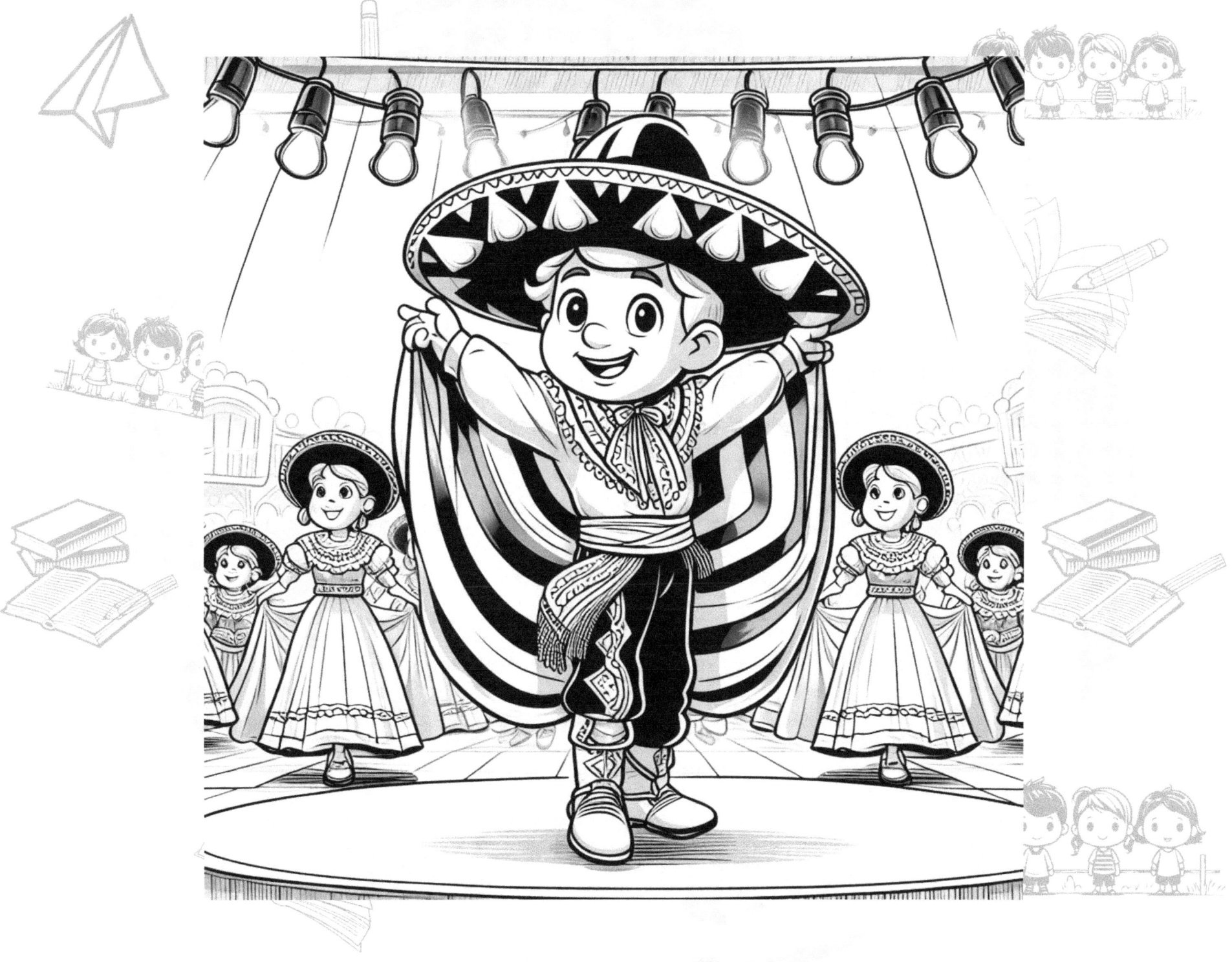

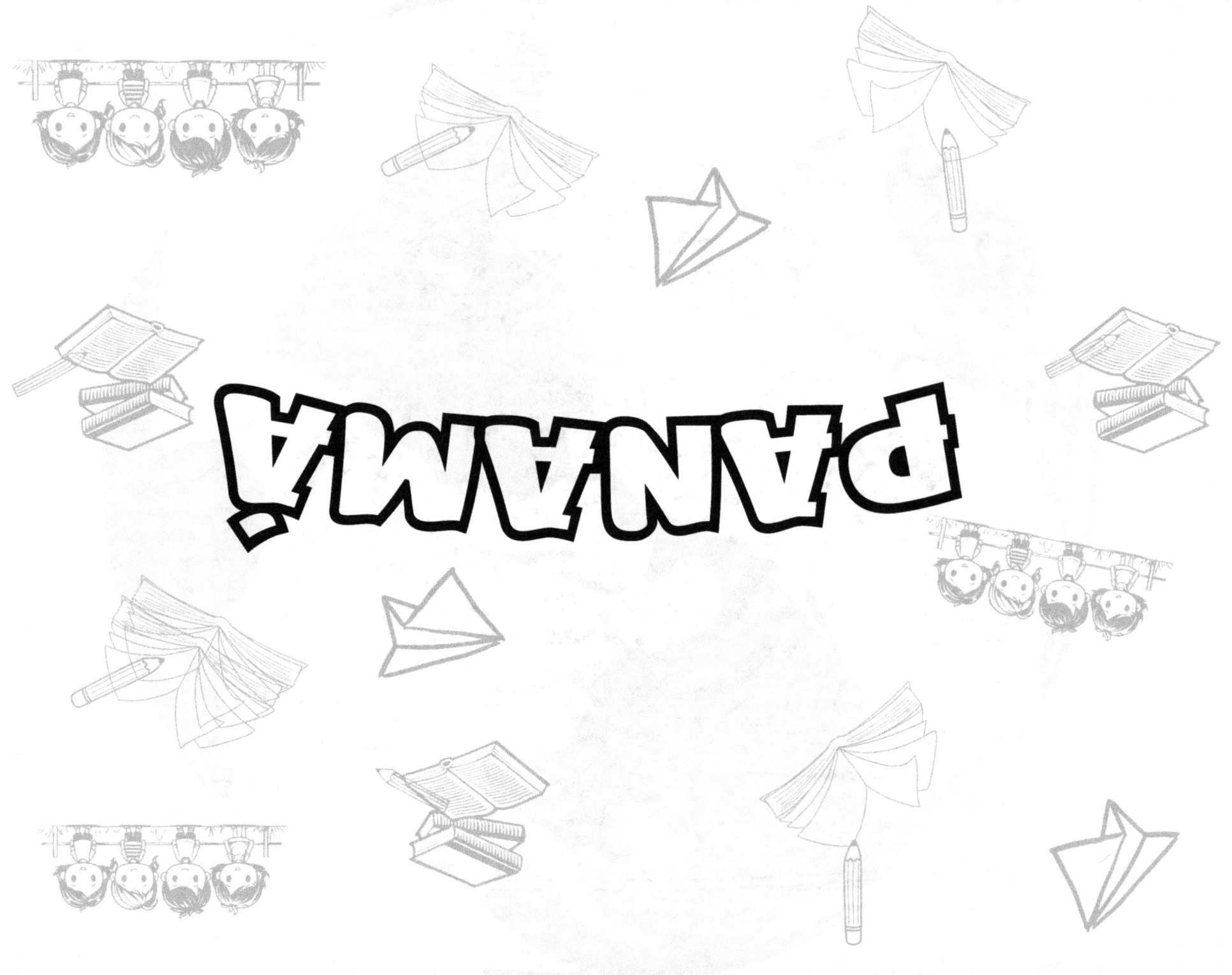

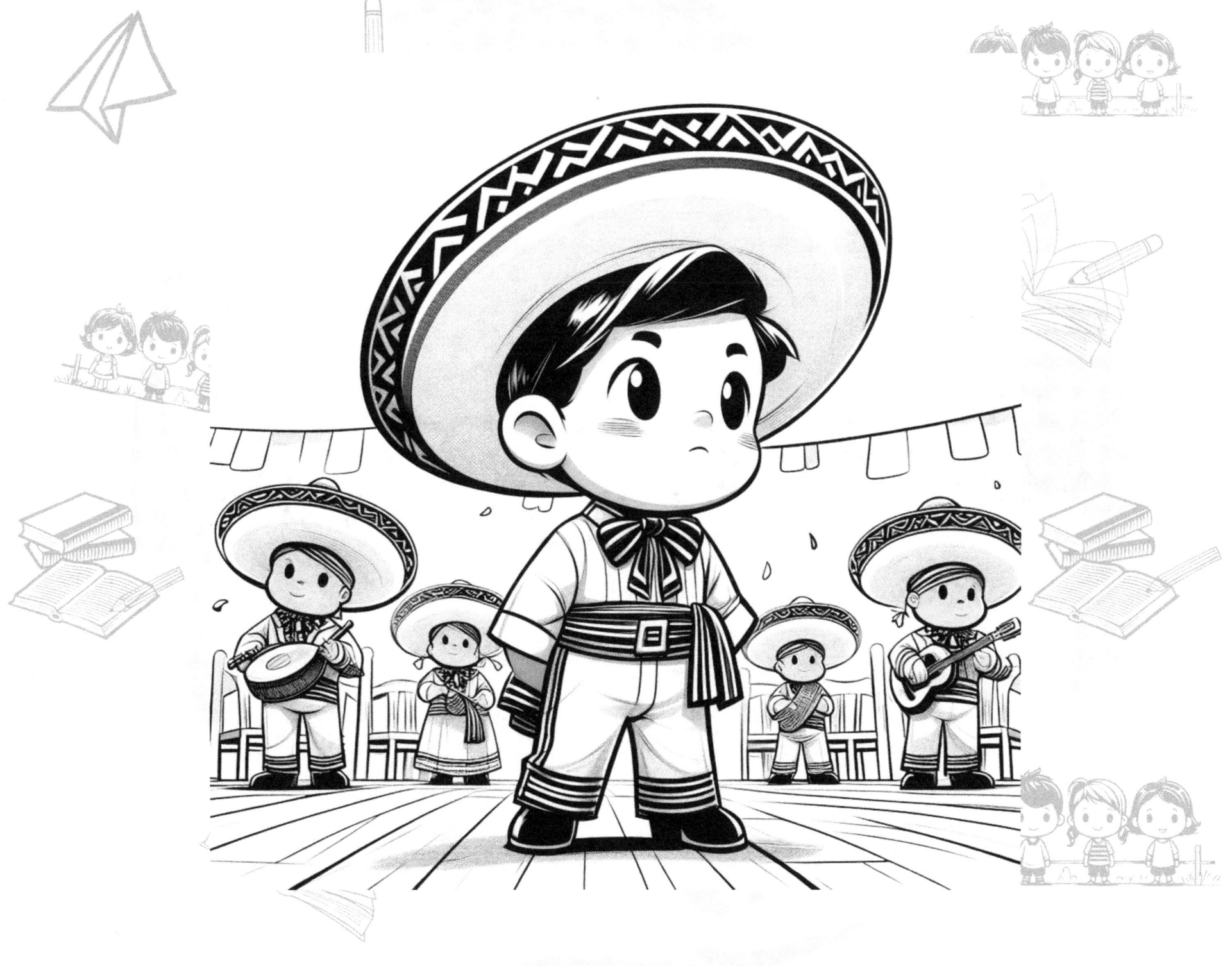

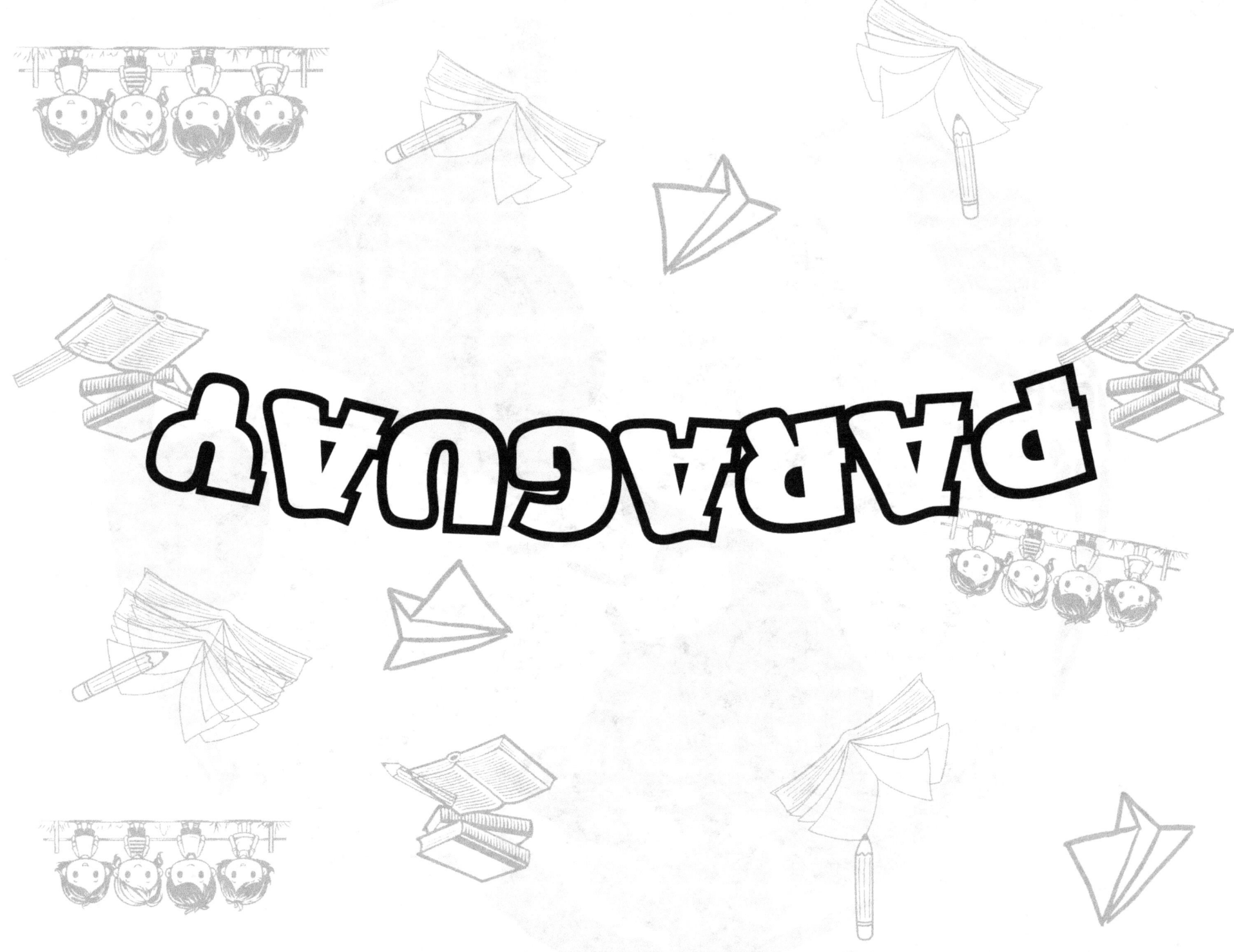

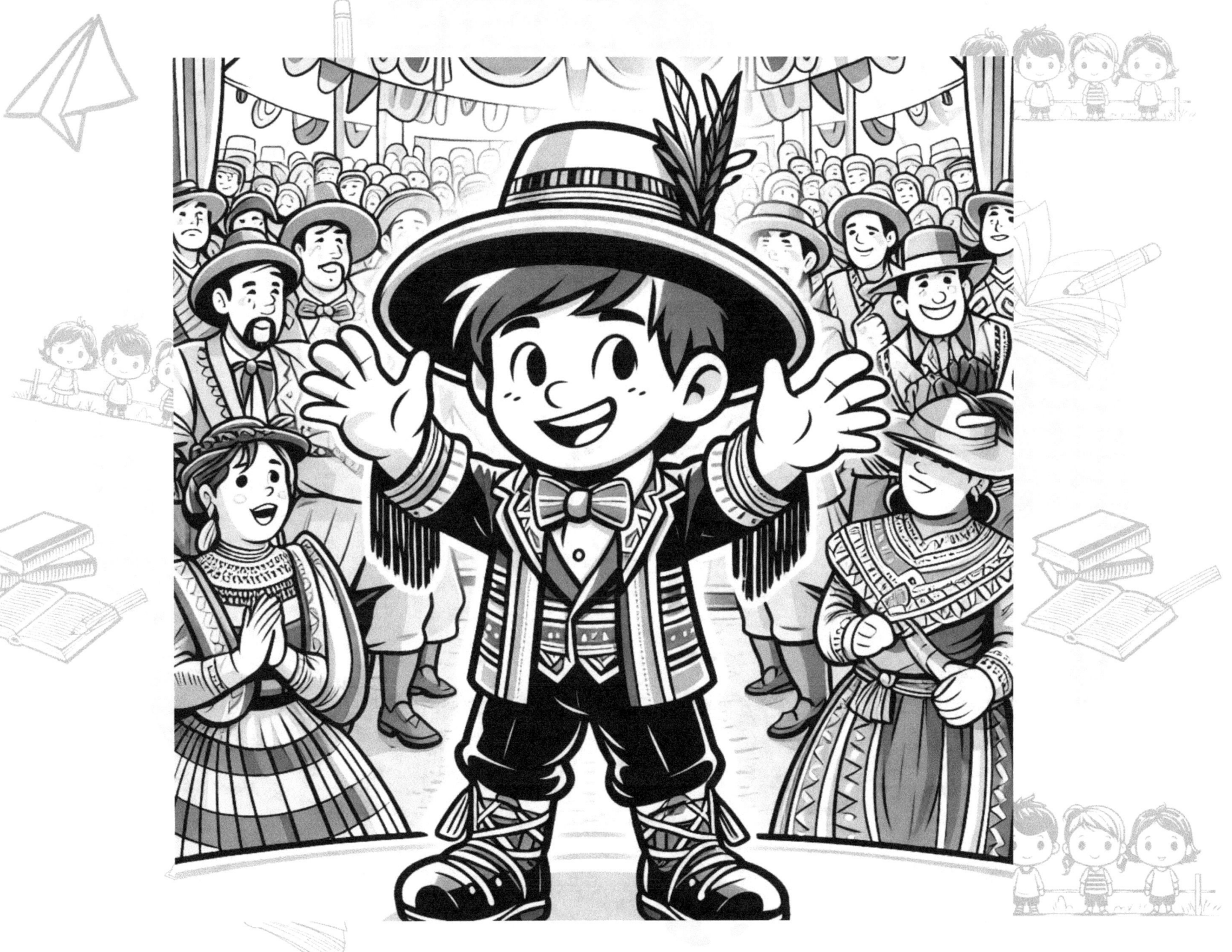

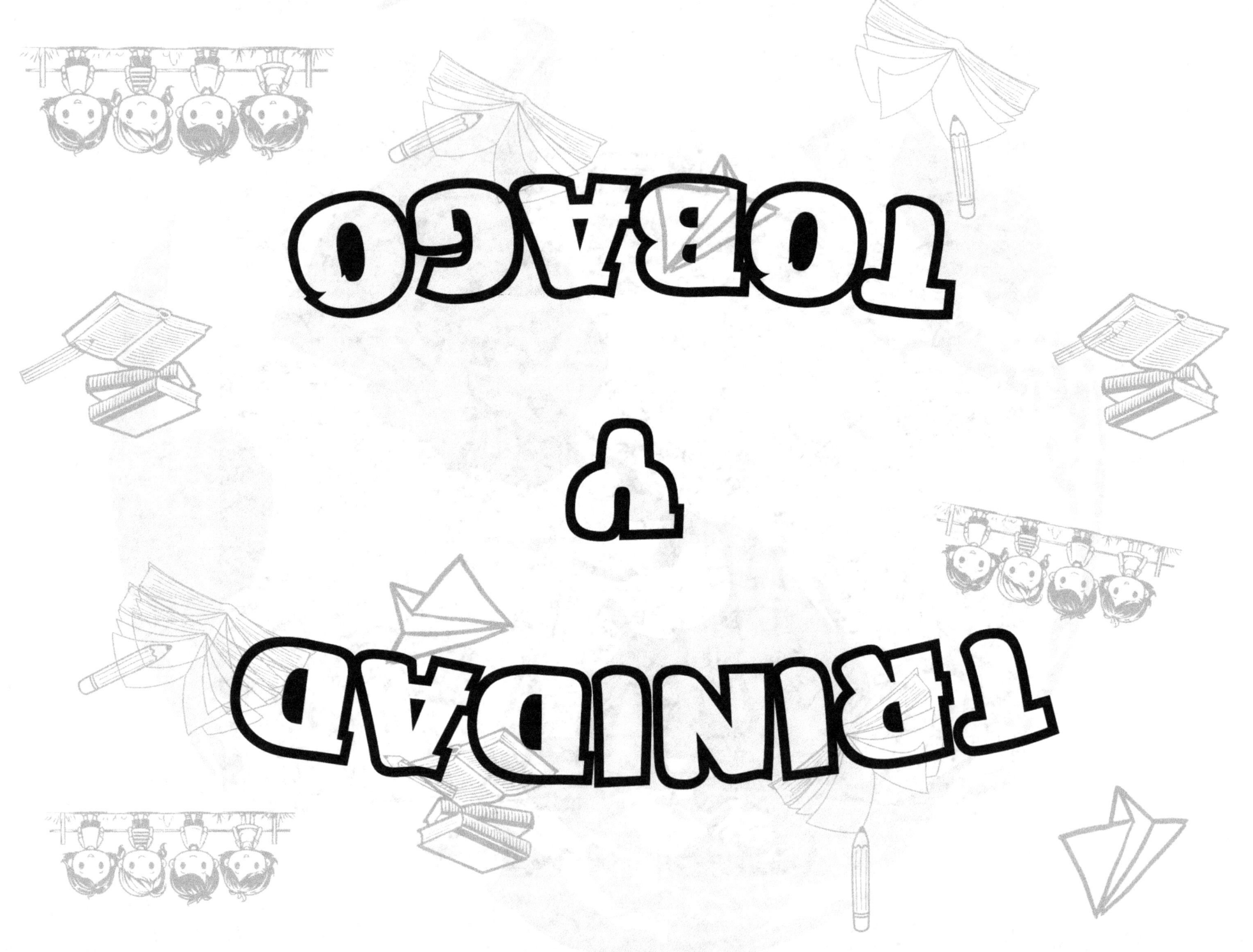

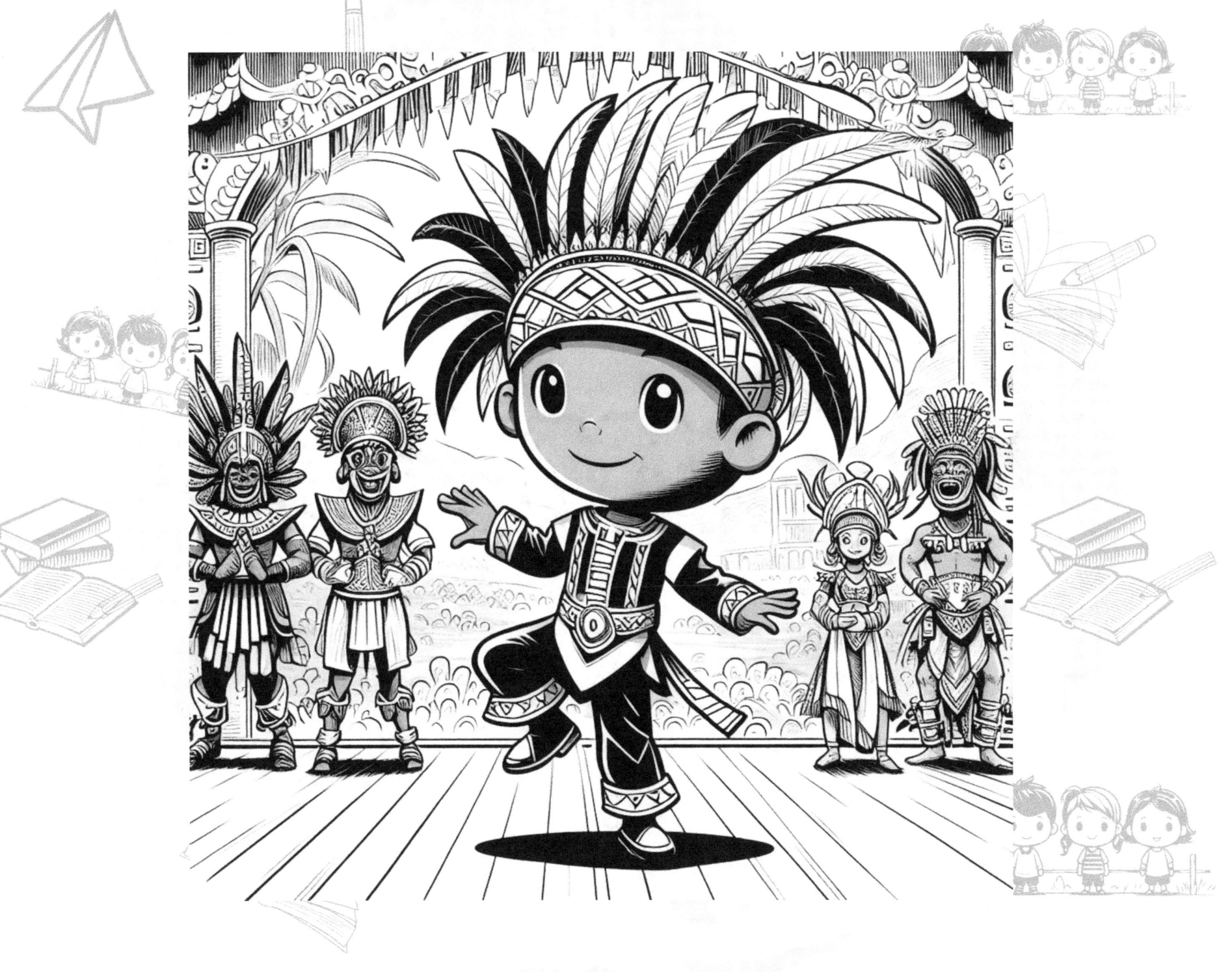

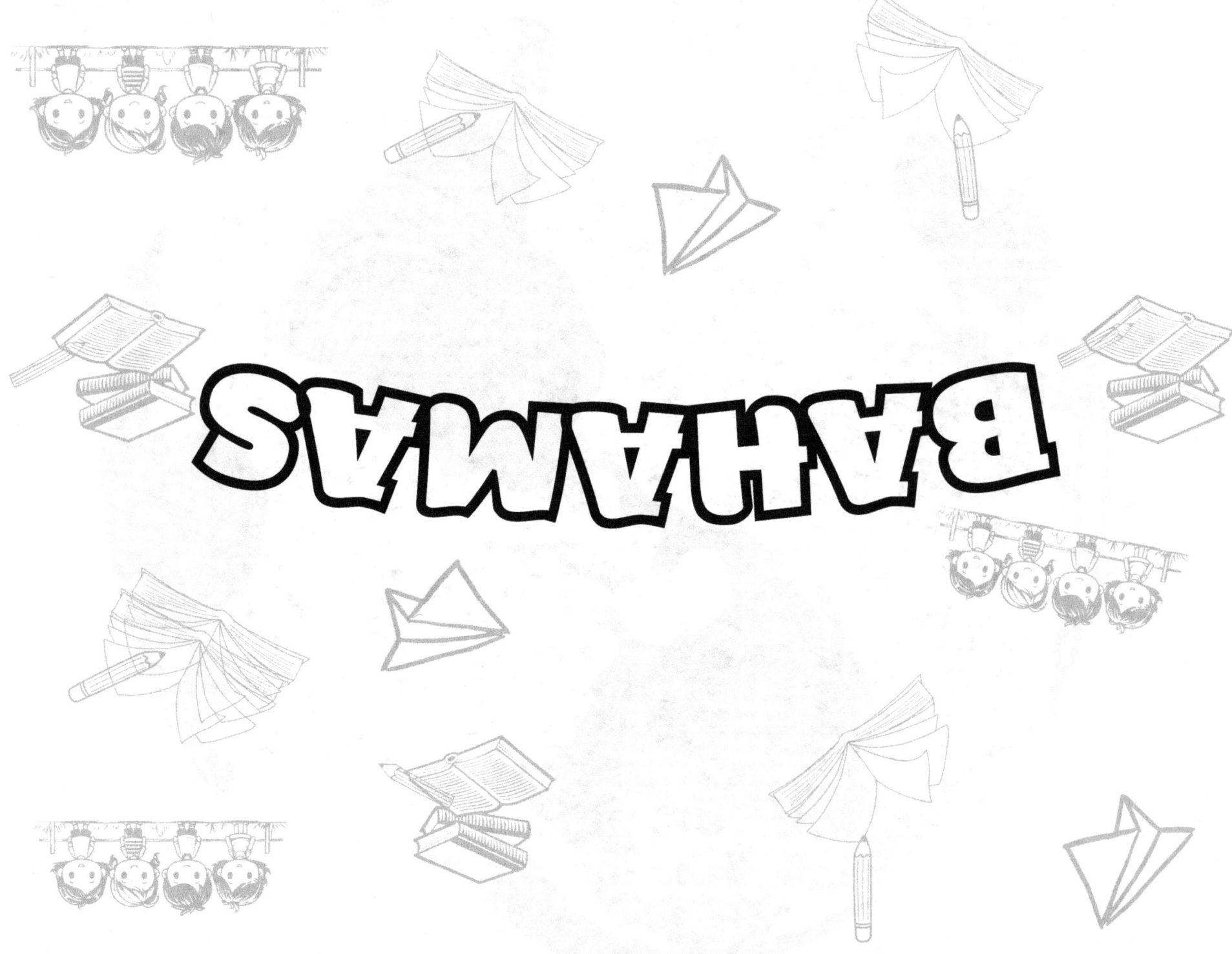

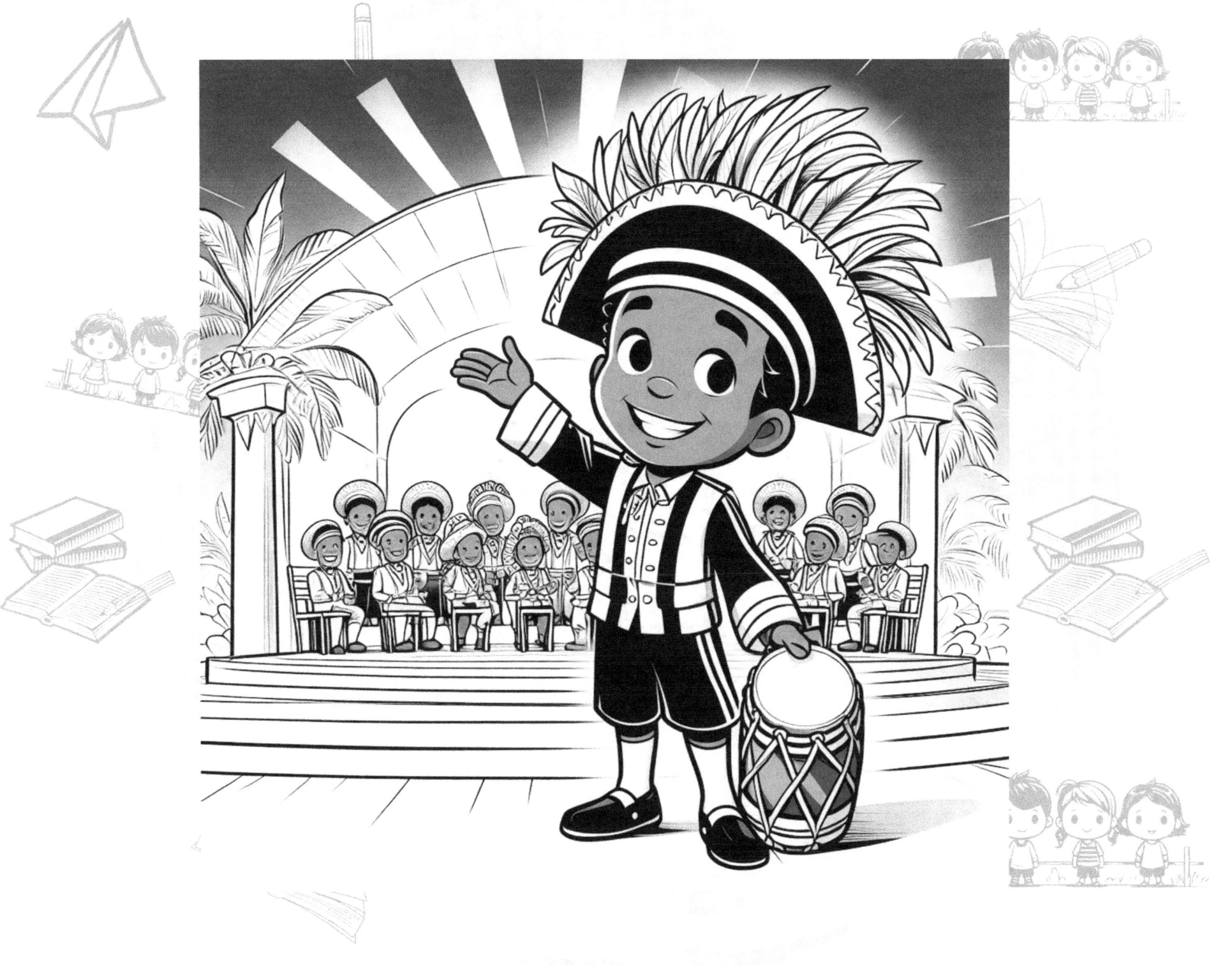

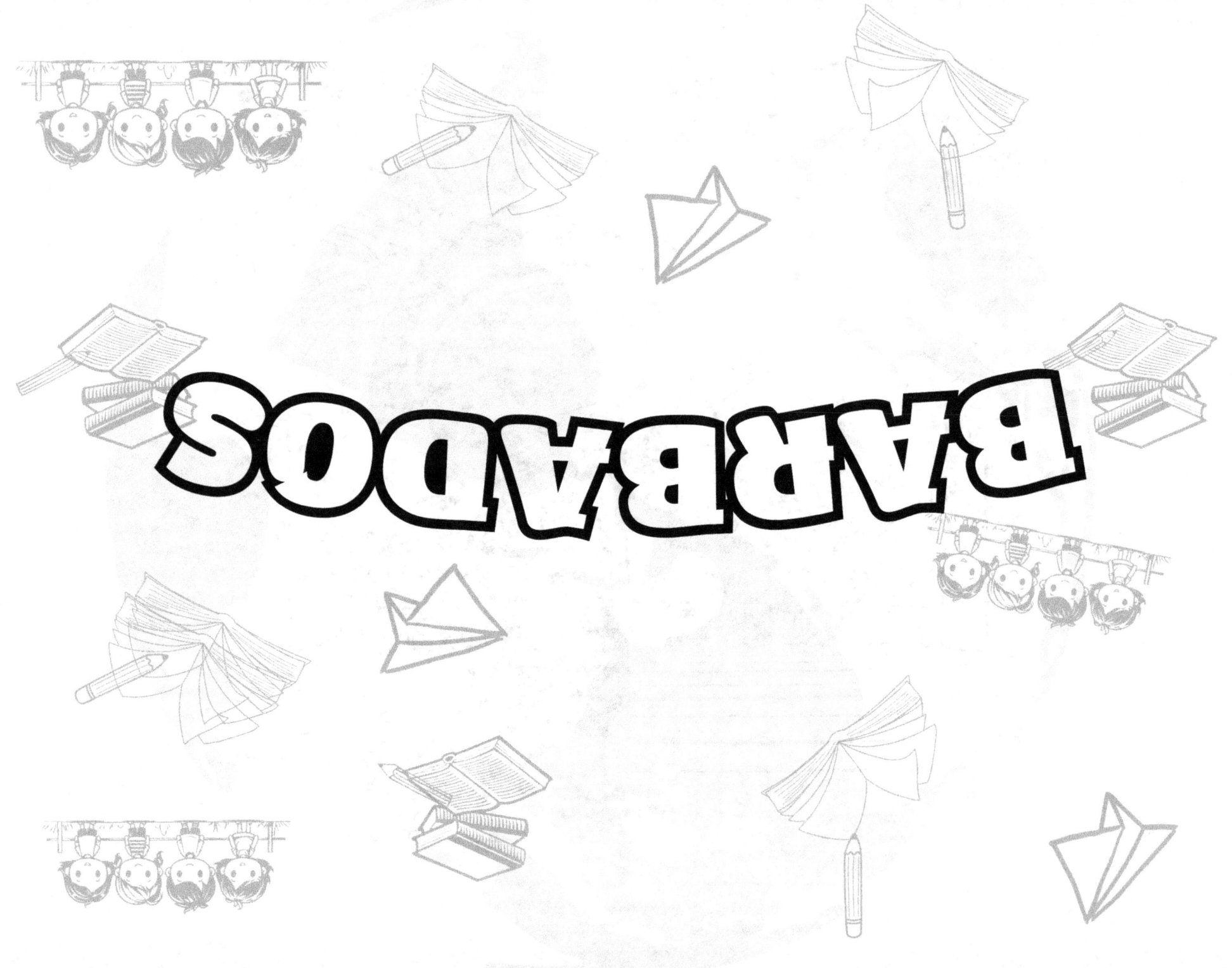

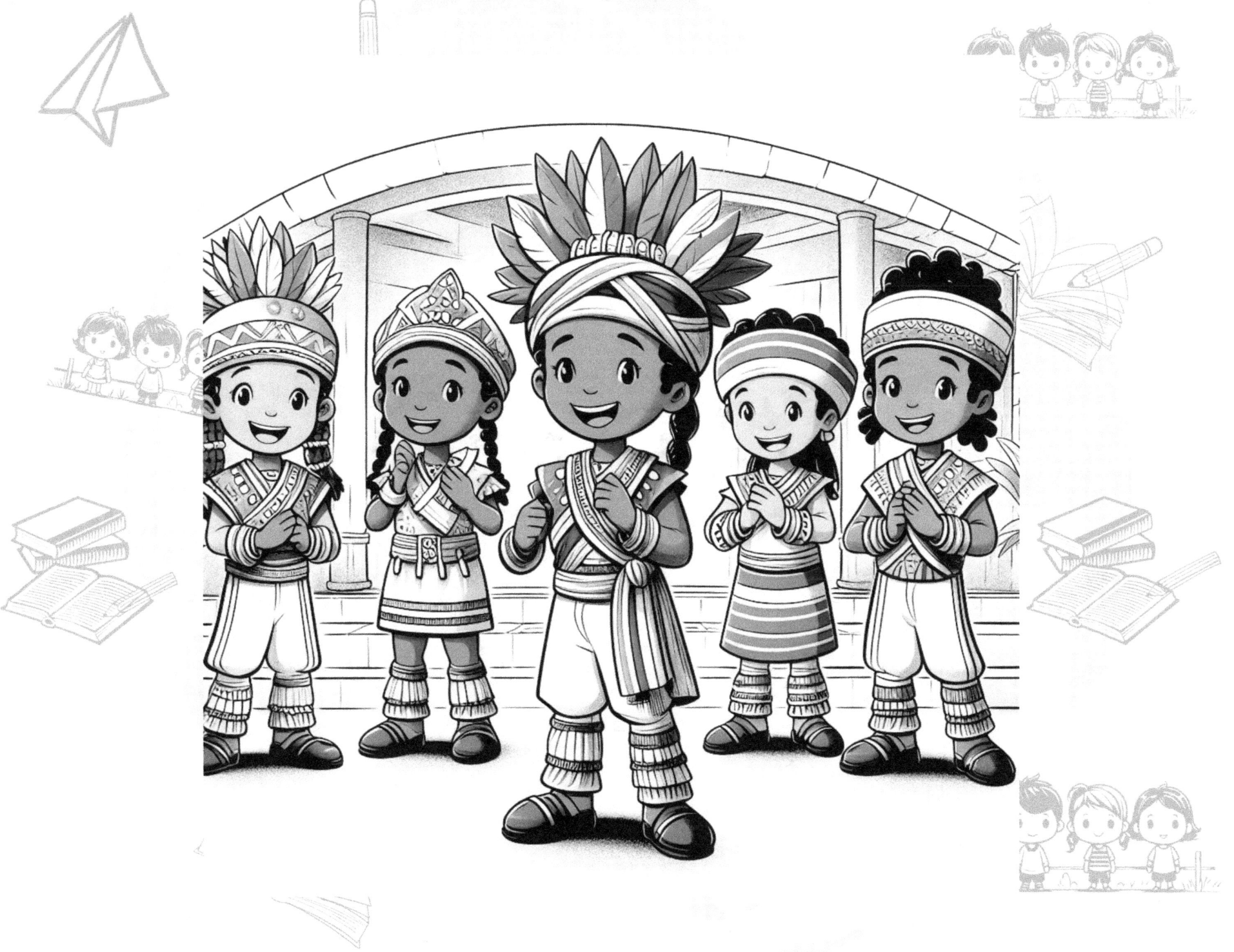

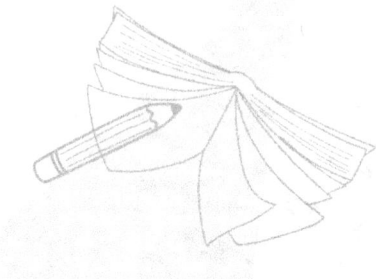
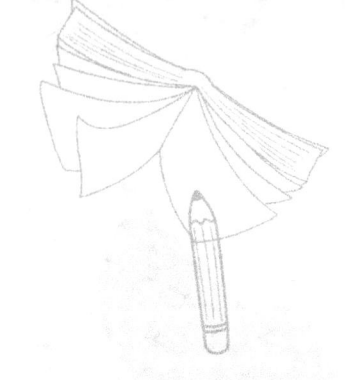
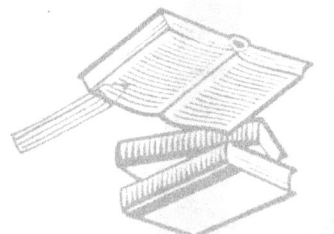
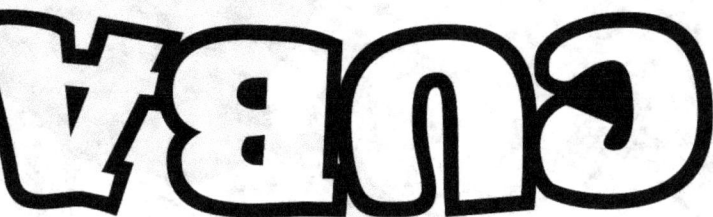

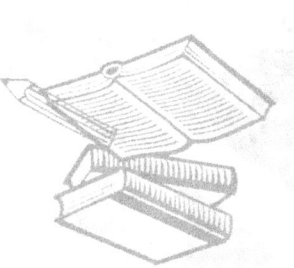
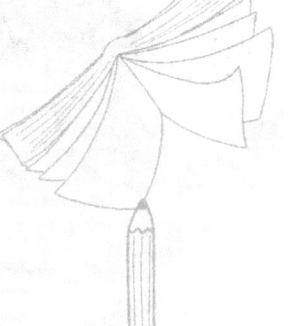
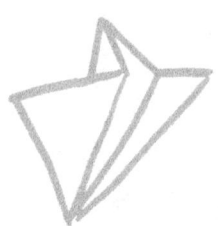
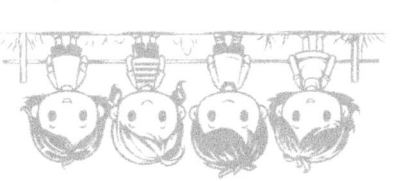

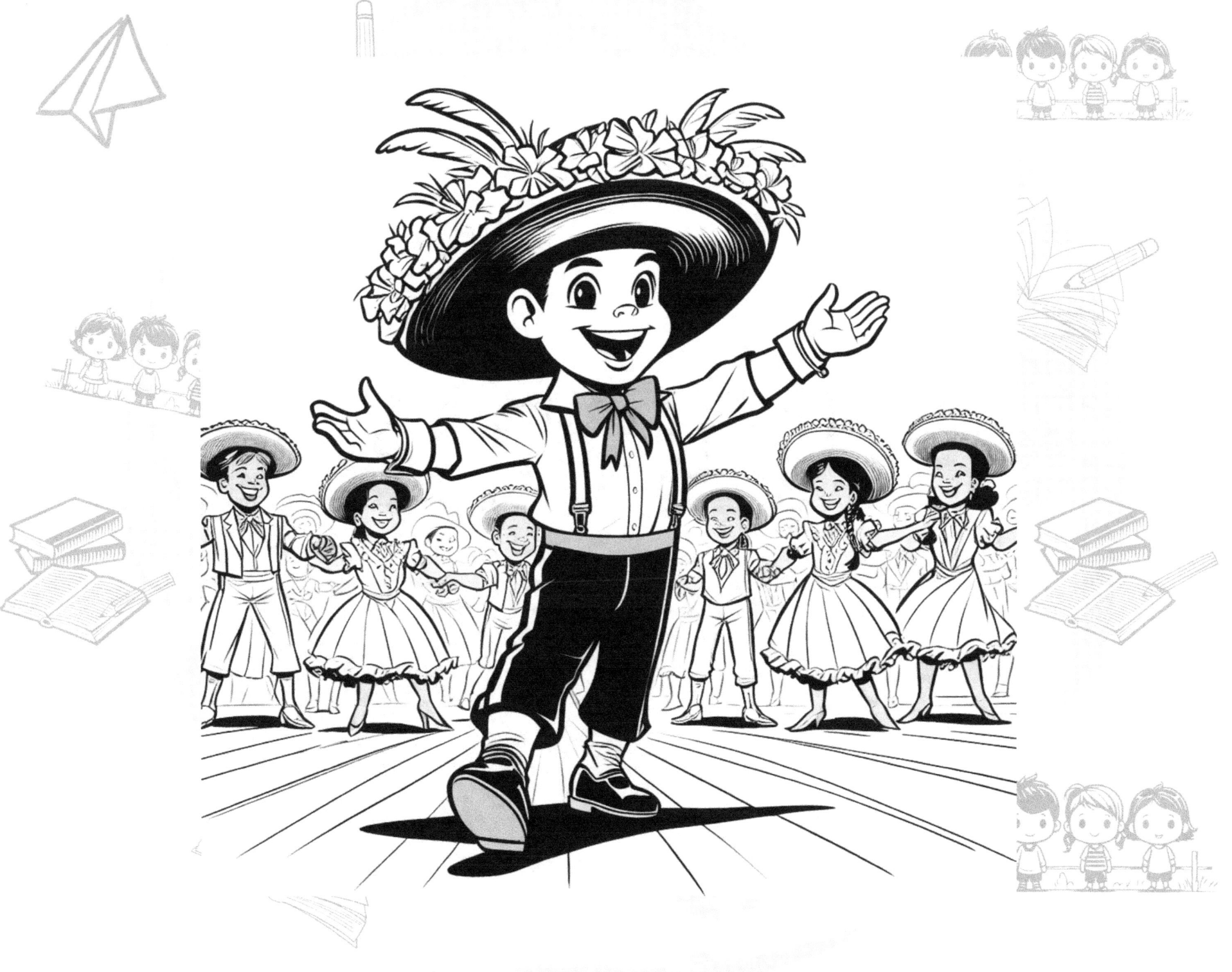

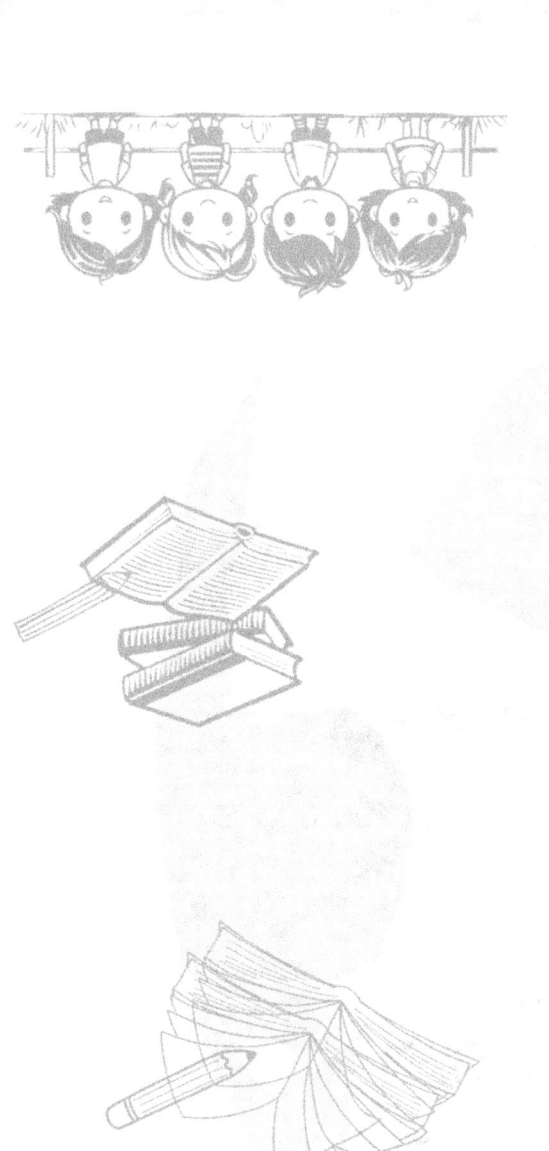
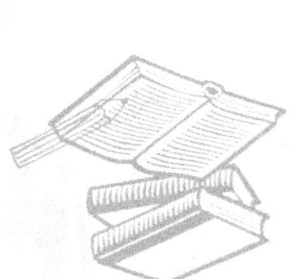
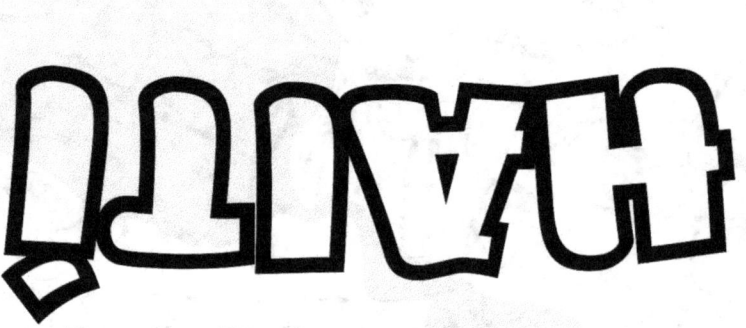
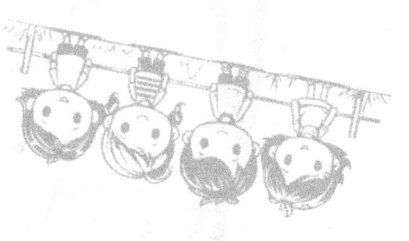

HAITI

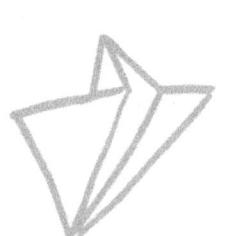

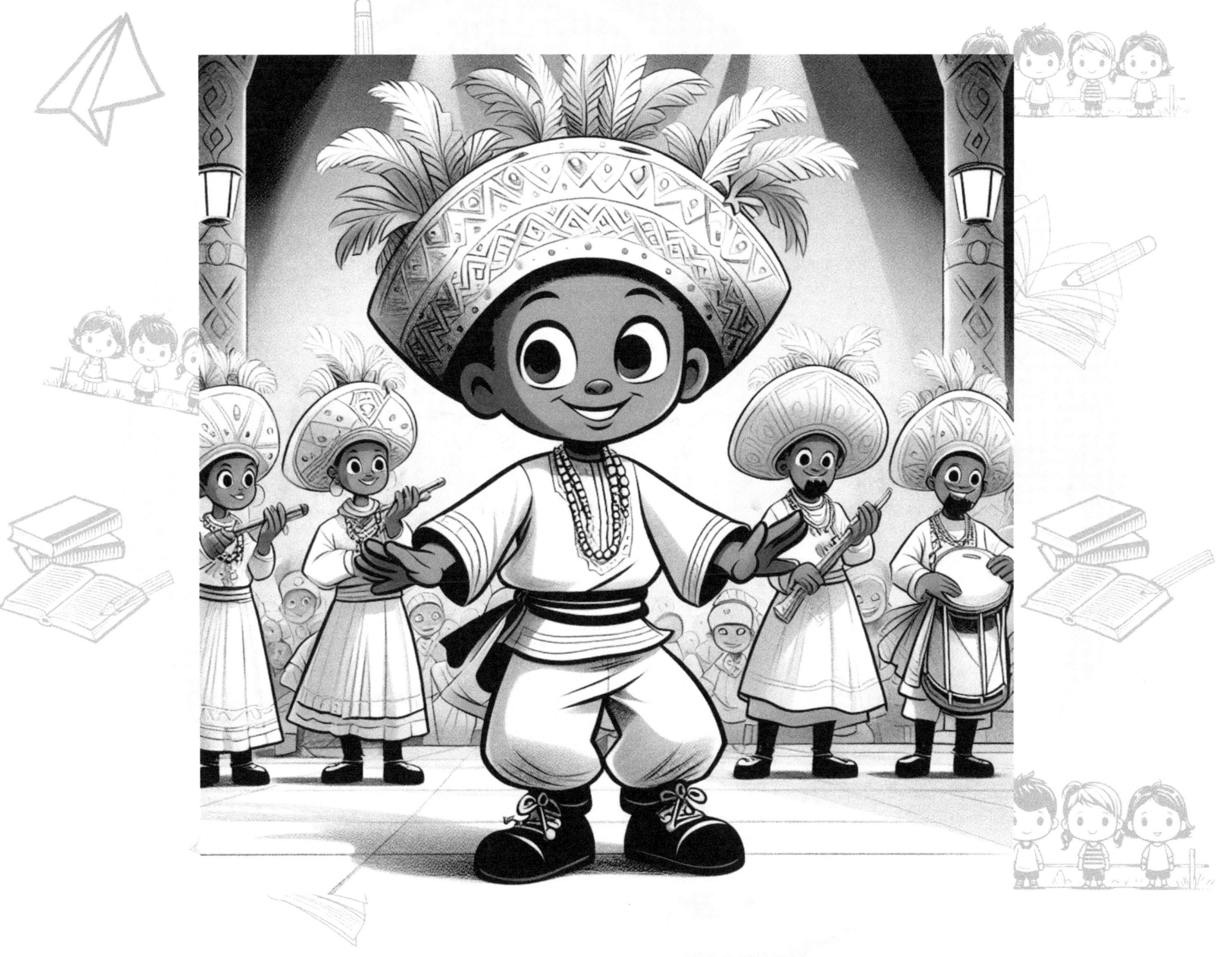

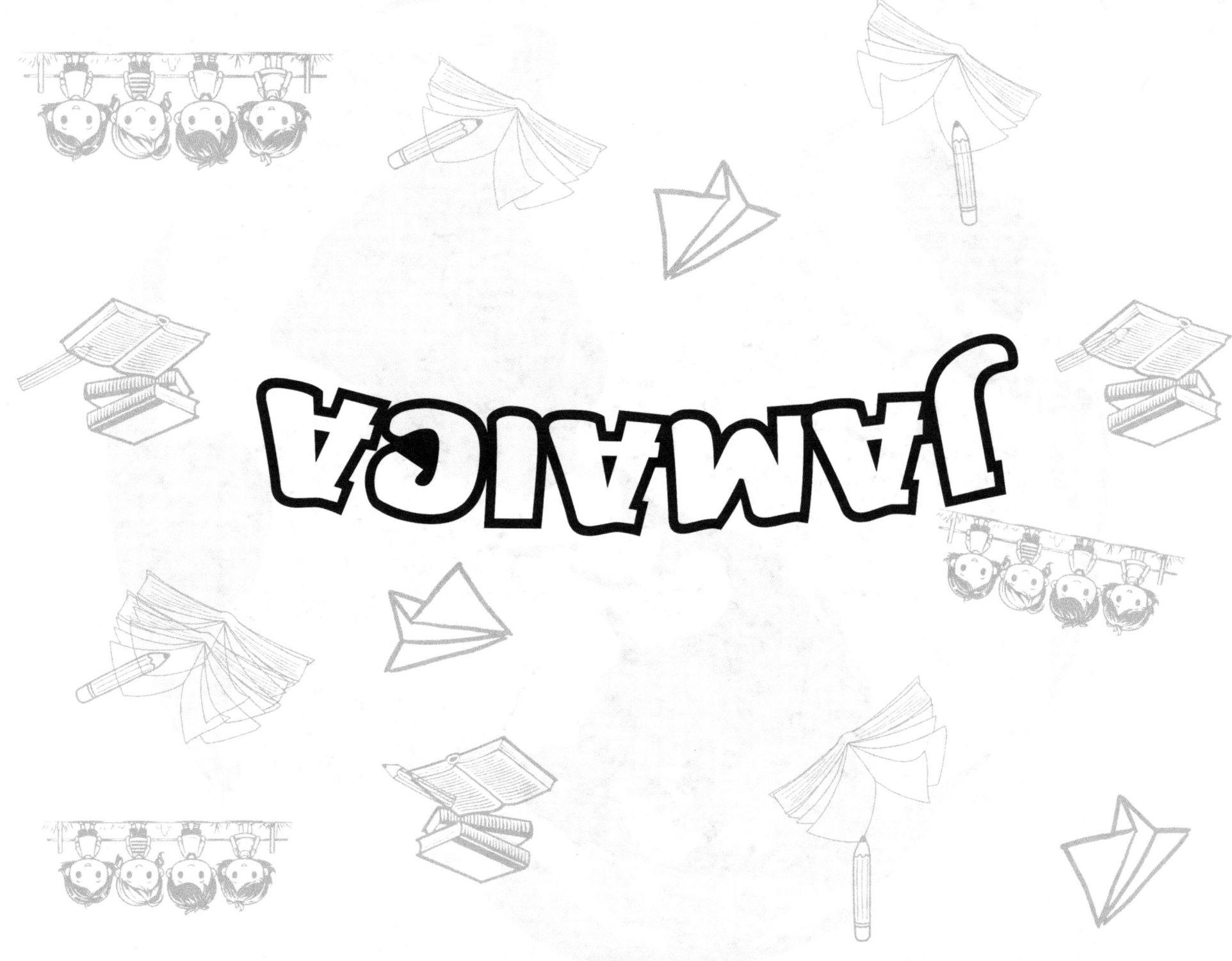

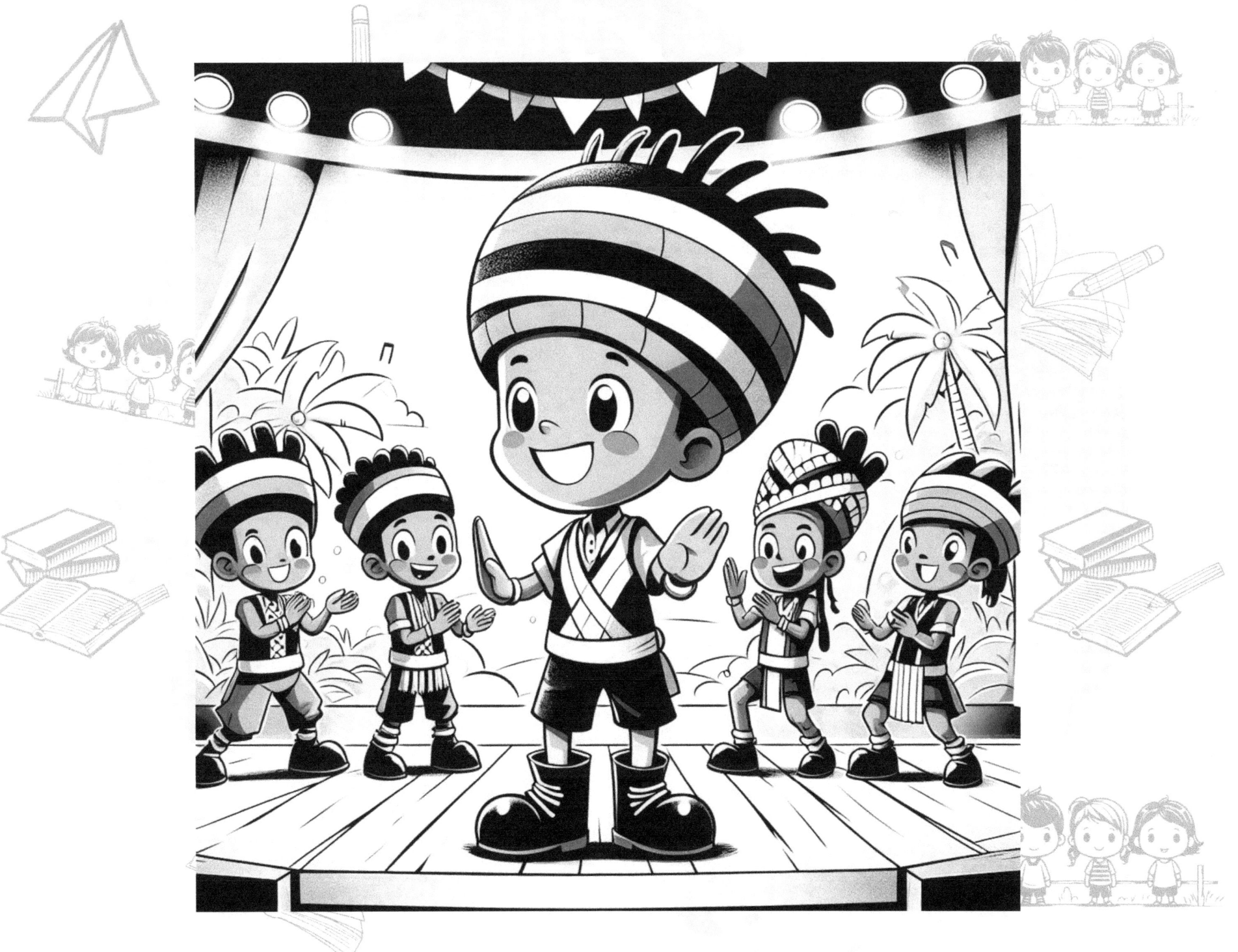

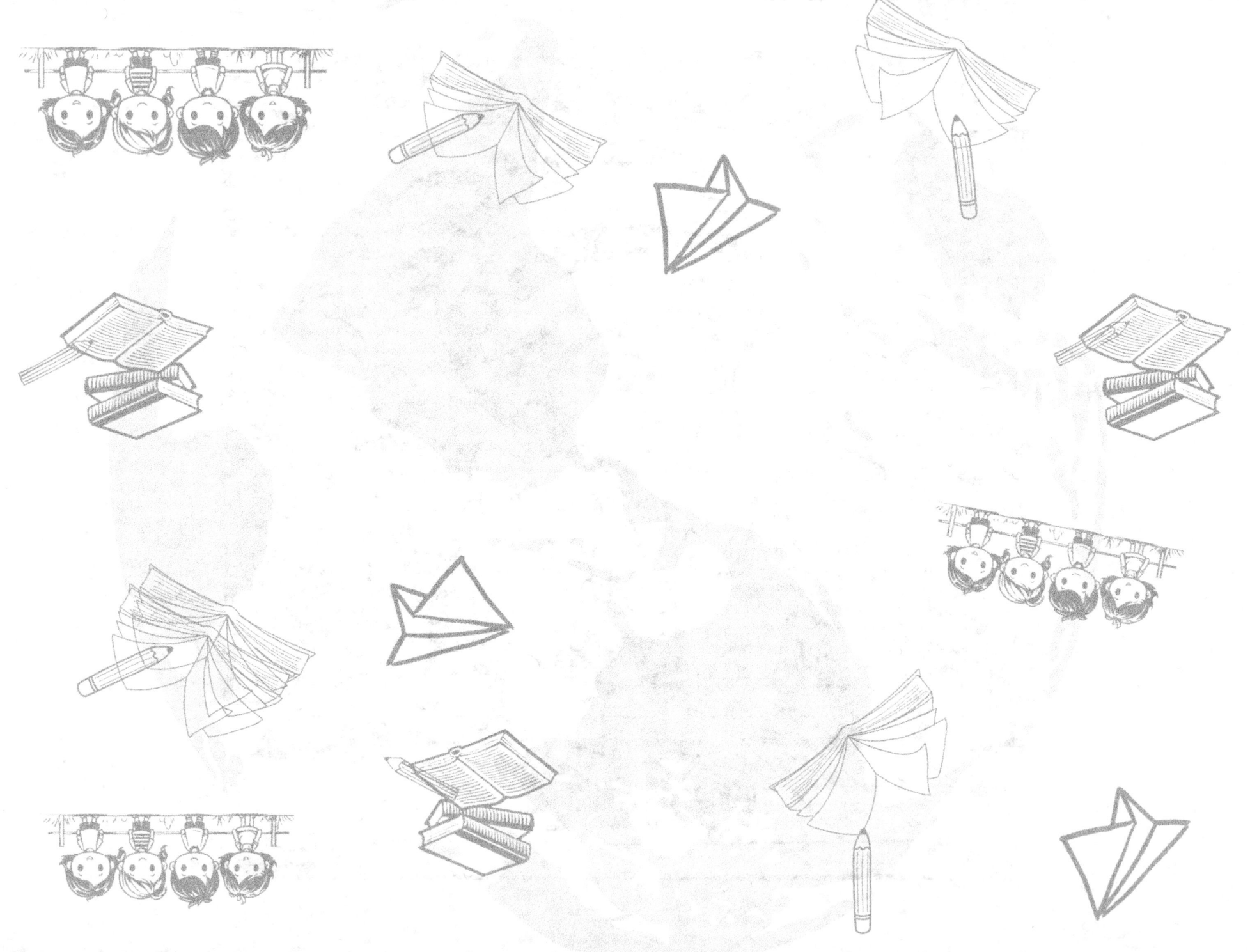

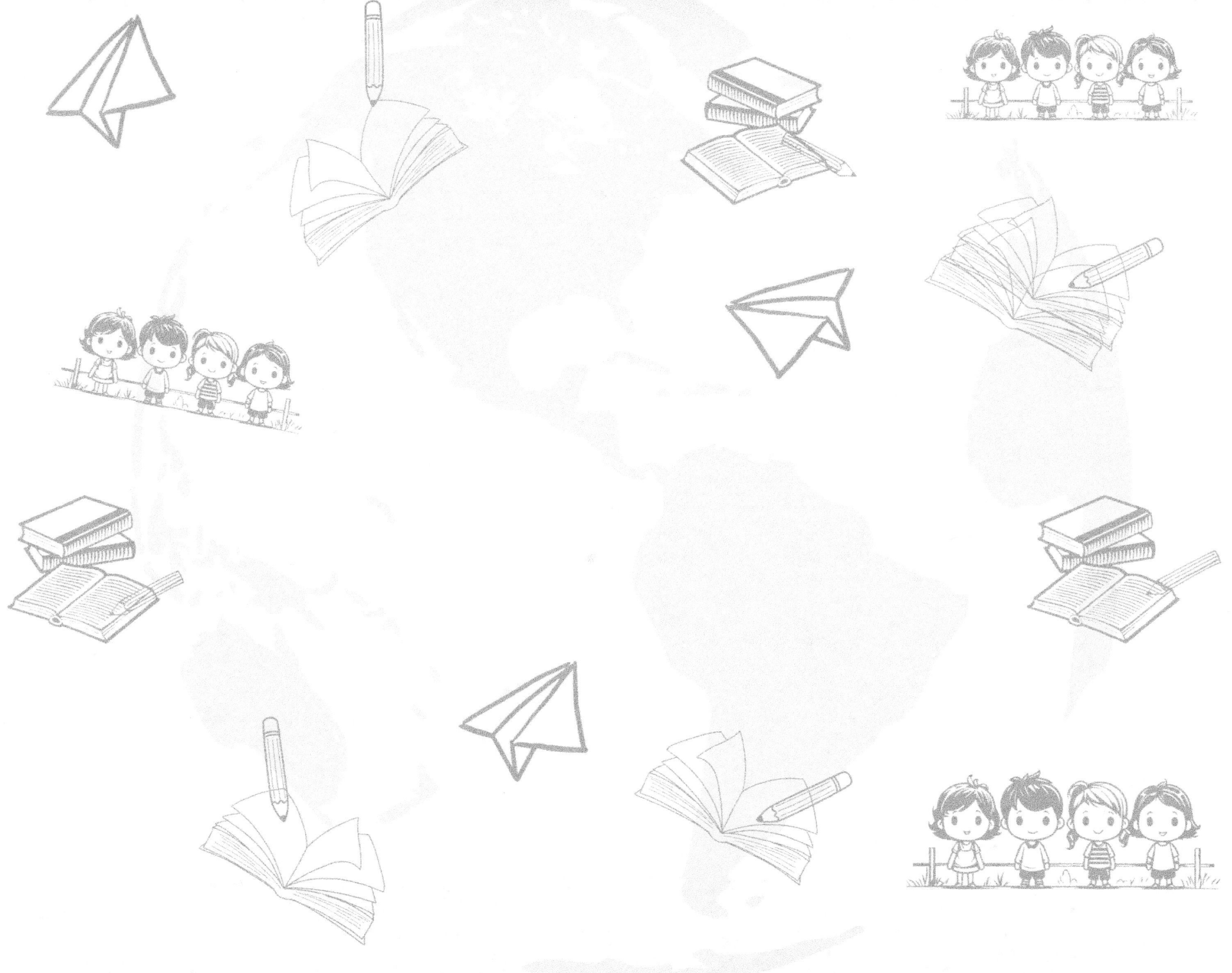